Betty Crocker's PARTY BOOK

Illustrated by Anne and Harlow Rockwell

ISBN: 978-0-470-38625-5
Facsimile Edition 2009

We're excited to bring you this treasured edition of Be
exactly as they appeared in the original 1960 cookbook.
years, so you will want to use today's ingredients and m
safety concerns have also changed over the years, so be
making Marshmallow Frosting (page 43).

D1058864

... ...ites when

WILEY

Dear Hostess,

Everybody loves a party, and if you are like most of our friends you want yours to be very special. You want a party to be proud of, whether it's large or small, for children or for grown-ups. So we have planned this book to help you with your parties through the year.

As you browse through these pages you'll find help in planning ahead, as well as ideas for decorations, games, favors, menus, and recipes for every kind of special occasion. There are pages and pages of parties -- birthday parties for children of all ages, parties for every holiday, and parties for the bride from the first shower to the silver and golden anniversaries.

If you will turn first to this book every time you entertain, I promise that your party will be fun for you as well as for your guests.

Cordially,

Betty Crocker

Contents

What Makes a Hostess Famous

Through the ages, a gathering of family and friends has been considered the best way to celebrate special occasions like birthdays, weddings, anniversaries, and holidays—or just to welcome friends. Parties give an opportunity to plan for the pleasure of loved ones and friends. A successful party leaves fond recollections of the occasion.

In fact, parties are an essential part of family life—whether they be fancy or simple, for many or few, for family or friends. Whatever the occasion, they often become a part of the family tradition.

If you would like to be known for the parties you give, there is really no secret: just invite congenial people and entertain them graciously. It sounds easy and it is—when you know how.

If you recall the parties you enjoyed most, you will find that they all possess basic similarities:

Everyone at the party was relaxed, including the host and hostess.

The setting for the party was attractive and arranged so that meeting others was easy.

All activities took place with seemingly little effort.

The food served was appropriate to the occasion, attractive, and delicious.

On leaving you said with all sincerity, "Thank you for inviting me to your lovely party."

To make a party "come alive" requires careful planning ahead of time:

What sort of party? A dinner? A brunch? A tea? Here consider the time of year, your space and facilities for entertaining, your budget, and your personal preference. The sort of party will determine the decoration, the selection of music and food.

Why? There need not be a special reason for a party—perhaps it's just an excuse to break up a long winter. But if there is a holiday, birthday, or vacation trip in the offing, or newcomers that you'd like to meet your friends, by all means adapt this theme to your party plans.

Who? People are the basic ingredient of parties, so plan the guest list carefully. Remember to consider hobbies, special interests, age, and even disposition in inviting guests who may not know each other well.

When? Consider which day and time would be best for your guests. Week-end parties are best for working couples. Couples with young children might prefer a late dinner hour which gives them time to tuck the children in bed before leaving home. Parties for school children are usually planned for after-school hours, ending with a light meal.

Where? At your home, of course. The amusement room is well suited to very informal entertaining or for children's parties. The living room and dining room are ideal for sit-down dinners or buffet service for a larger group. In mild weather the patio becomes an extra place to hold parties. Be sure space is adequate for the number of guests invited. When there's a special occasion like a visit to the zoo or a new play opening, plan refreshments at home afterwards.

This chapter is devoted to giving you special help in making party giving easier: details on planning, adding zest to foods with herbs and spices, brightening your table with interesting accessories, and how to store accessories so they are fresh and readily available for use again.

We hope this will prove to be the kind of book you will use for information or inspiration when looking for ways to entertain—from 8-year-olds to loved ones on a 50th wedding anniversary.

The Importance of Planning

The second step in party planning is making the lists: the guests, meal plan, shopping, and even china and accessories. Snatch a few moments to fill out these lists and file them away for handy reference as work on the party progresses. Another handy list shows last minute duties from the arrival of the first guests to the serving of the food. Be sure that each member of the family understands the part he is to play.

GUEST LIST

Invite guests well ahead of time, contacting them by phone or by note, as you wish. Keep your guest list by the phone to mark acceptances, regrets, who will be late, or who needs directions.

MEAL PLANNING

Planning a delicious meal that's simple to serve and yet just different enough to boost your hostess rating is a challenge for most homemakers.

Think of these things when you plan a party meal:

Ahead-of-Time Preparation: Try to choose foods that can be prepared the day before, the morning of, or at least an hour before the party. If you have a freezer, you can prepare some food a week or more ahead. You'll find that almost every menu in this book has some foods that can be made ahead. If you are intrigued by a new recipe, try it first on the family.

Guests' Likes: If you know your guests' food likes and dislikes (or allergies), take them into account in menu planning.

Here are a few rules to follow in planning meals for both entertaining and everyday:

Variety of Textures: This is a *must*, and makes the difference between an inspired cook and an ordinary one. The Chinese are past masters of this art in combining chewy foods, such as almonds or fried noodles, with smooth sauces and softer foods. You'll find variety of texture in the menu suggestions throughout this book.

Color: Think of different foods as colors on an artist's palette—all ready for you to put into a picture. What a change takes place on a dinner plate of white baked fish and mashed potatoes when you add a green vegetable like broccoli and garnish the fish with lemon and parsley!

Variety: Serve both hot and cold foods at every meal. Even on the hottest summer days, serve one hot food with the cool foods you find so refreshing (it's better for digestion, too).

It's best to plan different sorts of foods in your meals. For example, if you are having cream pie for dessert, vegetable soup is a better choice than a cream soup would be. Try to avoid too many starches or too many protein foods in a single meal.

Contrast in Flavor: Mild-flavored bland foods complement highly seasoned or strong-flavored foods. For example, the Mexicans serve spicy enchiladas in tomato sauce with corn meal tortillas which are mild in flavor. It's best not to serve more than one strong flavored food (such as onions, cabbage, salmon, or salt fish) in the same meal. This same rule applies to highly seasoned food.

Simplicity: A few well cooked and seasoned foods, attractively served are much better than a table crowded with many hurriedly prepared foods.

Flavor Mates: Certain foods seem to go together naturally: pork with apples and sweet potatoes; veal with tomatoes; chicken with cranberries; lamb with mint; egg and cheese dishes with green vegetables.

Many of these rules or principles may be an instinctive part of your cooking habits already. But to really master the art of food, refer to these concepts when you're planning and serving. You will find yourself developing into a more creative cook each day.

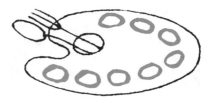

Variety Is the Spice of Life

To add your unmistakable touch of flavor to foods, there is no cooking art more worth perfecting than the fine art of adding herbs and spices.

Subtlety Is the Key Word: If you can taste an herb, you have used too much. Great cooks know that herbs and spices must be so subtly used that you can never distinguish one from the other. They must contribute to the food and blend with it in order to bring out its best flavor. They must never overwhelm or mask the taste.

Herbs—Fresh or Dried? Many people who have eaten fresh herbs prefer them to dried ones. But since tinned or bottled dried herbs are available all year 'round and fresh herbs are available only during the growing season, it is well to learn to cook with both. Herbs may be potted and brought inside for a winter herb garden in a sunny window. Sweet marjoram, sweet basil, and thyme grow best indoors.

To Freshen Dried Herbs: Release the flavor by marinating the herb in the liquid to be used in the dish (broth, oil, or water), or by crumbling the herbs with fingertips in palm of hand.

Garlics for Salads and Sauces: Garlic has a subtlety and lightness that does tender things to salads. Garlic is meant to mingle with other herbs to enhance the flavor of beef or chicken, as in the spaghetti sauce (see p. 41).

What Herb or Spice Is Best with What Food? You can obtain from spice companies excellent herb and spice charts that suggest which herbs are best with different foods. Why not tape an herb chart inside your kitchen cupboard door for easy reference when cooking? Or you may frame a pretty herb chart to hang on the kitchen wall. In experimenting with herbs or spices, add them sparingly until you learn the amount that suits the taste of your family.

Spices: Of all food ingredients spices probably have the most romantic history. The finding, shipping, and selling of spices have built empires. In fact, America was discovered by men looking for a new route to the source of spices.

Their greatest use today, as in the past, is to make food more palatable. Some of the other ways in which spices are used are for their therapeutic properties in prescriptions (oil of cloves), as invaluable dye-stuffs (turmeric and saffron), and as the base of perfumes and ointments.

The most important of all spices is pepper. Its importance is based on its ability to strengthen and bring out the flavor of almost any food with which it is mixed. The classic spices besides pepper include paprika, mustard, cinnamon, cloves, ginger, allspice, and nutmeg.

Why not try adding mace to chicken casseroles, coriander to pea soup, caraway to lamb stew, or poppy seed to poultry stuffing? For other ideas, consult the spice charts mentioned earlier.

To be assured of fresh spices you may buy the whole seed (such as black pepper or whole nutmeg) and grate or grind as needed. If you buy powdered spices, select as small a container as possible, and be sure the containers are tightly closed when not in use.

FOOD CAN BE A CONVERSATION PIECE

The hostess who is famous for her parties is often the first to serve a new dish . . . or a new variation of an old favorite. She always tries to choose one food as the conversation piece of the meal.

Intriguing new party foods don't just happen. This hostess is probably an avid recipe collector who has worked out a system of filing the interesting recipes clipped from magazines and newspapers and of preparing them for her family. Once tried and passed by the family, the new recipe is ready for a party.

FILE NEW RECIPES

If you are like most homemakers, you do clip recipes now and then, usually sticking them into a cluttered kitchen drawer and seldom, if ever, trying or using them. Why not resolve today to go through that drawer and file the really promising recipes in a separate "To Be Tried" file card box? Or start a collection of recipes and homemaking hints in a loose leaf notebook like the *Betty Crocker Notebook*.

One young homemaker friend of ours files new recipes in an expanding file marked with her own special headings. Besides the usual food categories like Meats and Vegetables, she has categories for Food Arrangement, Centerpieces, Herbs, and Garnishes. She clips and saves whatever interests her in cooking and homemaking.

When her Foreign Foods file was bursting, this mother started a series of foreign dinners for family and friends.

We suggest trying a new recipe each week. Unfamiliar foods presented more often may cause children to wonder, as with one young boy who asked, "Mommy, is this good, or is it one of your 'spearmints'?"

KEEP A PARTY NOTEBOOK

Many an experienced hostess saves her party menus together with the guest lists and shopping lists for future reference. A little note as to who liked some food especially and who takes cream or sugar in their coffee, can make you an even more thoughtful and considerate hostess at your next party.

BE A SMART SHOPPER

With the menu planned and on the kitchen bulletin board, it's time to write out the grocery list. Consult your recipes so you won't forget any ingredients; check the amounts of staples, too.

SELECTING SERVING DISHES

The jobs of planning a party meal and of choosing serving dishes go hand in hand. The homemaker with a sparkling new set of parfait glasses will be searching her cook books for an elegant ice cream parfait, while the woman who owns no soup bowls will surely plan chips and dip or salad as the appetizer for her dinner party.

Early in your party planning career you may find it helpful to completely set the dinner or buffet table with empty dishes—just to make sure everything fits and looks well.

Choosing Accessories

Make the choosing of accessories for your parties a real adventure. If you are using a theme for your party, choose accessories accordingly. For example, fish-shaped serving dishes help make a festive occasion of a family dinner (pictured on p. 72).

Versatile Accessories: We might all take a lesson from the Chinese in adapting accessories from any part of the house as either centerpieces or serving pieces.

Salad Bowl Set: Use a large salad bowl for fruits or hot rolls for large parties. Use individual bowls for nut dishes or sauce dishes.

Large Chop Plate or Tray: Use one as a platter for a large party; center with a matching bowl as chip and dip tray.

Pitchers of All Sorts: They are for beverages, of course; and also make graceful flower containers or, with imagination, a table centerpiece (p. 144).

Clear Glass Bowls: Float flowers or candles in one at each place at a dinner party; or use as finger bowls.

Cake Stand: This holds a violet centerpiece (p. 36) or a decorated cake (p. 69) with equal ease.

Compote Dishes: A large one can hold a holiday fruit and flower arrangement (p. 115); small ones are nice for sauces and candies.

Snifters: Large ones hold lots of popcorn or cookies (see p. 141). For a dramatic dessert, fill the snifter with alternate layers of colorful ice creams and fresh or frozen fruits. As decoration, fill the snifter with floating flowers or an Easter egg nest.

ANTIQUES LEND CHARM

Have you noticed how many antique dishes seem to be finding their way into food service material and fashionably set tables today?

Old Pie Plates: For popping hot rolls right out of the oven and onto the table, what could be more appealing than the old-fashioned pottery or Bennington ware pie dishes? On one bargain hunting jaunt we found an old pie plate with a charming apple blossom design for 25c! Many times it has found its way to the table proudly holding biscuits, and they will stay piping hot.

Soup Tureens: These are wonderful for serving spaghetti at a buffet supper. The sauce can be kept hot in a chafing dish, to be poured over each serving of spaghetti, well drained and kept hotter in the tureen than in the usual shallow platter. Tureens are also good for chili or stew and are still the handsomest dishes for serving soup.

Old Coffee Pots: Whatever has happened to the custom of serving coffee from unusual pots? Perhaps for such a constantly viewed kitchen accessory, it would be wise to borrow some of the charm of yesterday. There are copper pots still to be found as handsome as the one shown here.

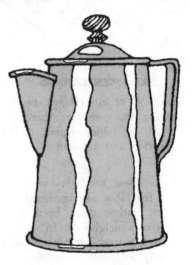

Salts and Peppers from Castors: If you like the tall beauty of antique crystal salts and peppers, you might rescue the old shakers from a now discarded castor set. They have an elegance rarely duplicated today.

TABLE CENTERPIECES

This center of interest will be the first thing your guests see when they approach the table, so plan it with imagination and ingenuity.

Flowers: These are every woman's choice for table arrangements. In summer, gather them from your garden or a neighbor's. In winter, make a few fresh-cut blooms go a long way with lots of greens. Ceramic figurines make attractive additions to flower arrangements. Or brighten artificial arrangements with silver or gold leaves (p. 60). A glossy-leafed green plant, in bloom or not, is another winter centerpiece idea.

For Children's Parties: Use the special decorated cake you've planned for dessert as the centerpiece. Some mothers prefer to serve children cupcakes, reserving the cake for a second party with grandparents, friends, and neighbors.

Flower Arranging Equipment: As suggested by a well known artist, these include:

    a round bowl
    a cylindrical vase
    a shallow oblong dish
    a bud vase
    a piece of slate (for dry
       arrangements)

Frogs, chicken wire, water-holding material such as Oasis, and flower shears are helpful, too.

PARTY TABLECLOTHS

The covering used on your table lends as much to the party mood as your accessories and centerpiece do.

Each holiday and each season has its own distinctive colors, so why not gather cloths in pretty colors to have ready for party meals?

If you're handy with a needle, you'll enjoy making the holiday cloths described in this book: Valentine Cloth (p. 57), Fish Net Cloth (pp. 73, 91), and Ruffled Buffet Table-cloth (p. 37). Make colored cloths yourself by hemming lengths of inexpensive washable plain-weave fabric. Or dye used white cloths holiday colors. Some homemakers have portable metal tables which they cover with colored single bed sheets for large family gatherings.

Runners: Bunny Runner (p. 78) or Christmas runner (p. 120) used over a white or light-colored cloth give a gay party feeling to your table. Runners also take the place of a centerpiece. And they take less space to store from year to year than cloths. Store runners and cloths clean but not starched or ironed. Roll them on cardboard cylinders from bolts of fabric.

Tray Mats: Both lap trays and "TV" trays, so popular for buffet dinners, can be given a party touch with tray mats of cloth or paper to match or contrast with the buffet tablecloth.

Storing Party Accessories: Party accessories and decorations take less space when neatly boxed.

Large cartons from your grocer, labeled by the season, can help you organize many items as follows:

Winter—Valentine and patriotic decorations

Spring—Easter decorations and artificial flowers

Summer—Fourth of July and picnic equipment

Fall—Thanksgiving decorations, gourds, and dried flowers

Christmas—Gift wrappings and lights as well as decorations

Birthdays and Anniversaries—Candles, special tablecloths, party games, and favors

Shelves or an old bookcase can be put to good use for these labeled cartons in either the attic, basement, or storage room. Keep one section clear for vases and other floral containers.

SERVING FOOD ATTRACTIVELY

Though food is usually arranged and garnished at the last moment before serving, arrangement and garnishing should not be a last-minute idea but as carefully planned as your whole meal. Wise hostesses know that eye appeal and appetite appeal go hand in hand.

Arrangement: Food arrangements may be circular or semi-circular, horizontal or vertical, symmetrical or asymmetrical. How much more appealing is a platter of pot roast with carrots, onions, and potatoes neatly arranged than with vegetables piled every which way?

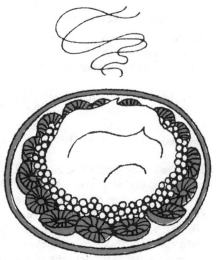

General Suggestions on Garnishes: A vegetable or fruit that complements the meat flavor is often the best choice for a garnish. Look at other foods in the meal for possible garnishes.

Garnishes usually should be edible.

Garnishes resembling birds or animals should be used only for children's parties.

Garnishes should not look handled.

Garnishes should be all ready for easy addition to the meat platter; they should be easy to serve onto dinner plates with the meat.

You may want to collect garnish ideas as you do recipes and file them in the appropriate categories in your recipe box.

SPECIFIC SUGGESTIONS FOR GARNISHING

Roast Turkey or Chicken: Surround with orange cups (half orange cleaned of fruit and membranes) filled with cranberry-orange relish or mashed yams. Or garnish with fruits and flowers (see p. 115).

Baked Ham: Arrange cream cheese-stuffed prunes in flower patterns, or pan-glazed pineapple slices on top of ham.

Pork Roast: Surround with tangy pink raspberry-applesauce in lettuce cups.

Chops: Since meat needs no carving, make it a platter meal. Garnish with bundles of asparagus spears or small whole green beans with pimiento "ties."

Roast Prime Ribs of Beef: Arrange broiled tomato halves at one end of platter; oven-browned potatoes, yams, or parsnips at the other end.

Vegetables: Heap mashed potatoes in the center of platter, and surround with green peas in turn surrounded with broiled mushroom caps.

Frankfurters: Party treatment like Frank-a-bobs (p. 93) becomes garnish. Serve franks arranged spoke-fashion on a round plate (p. 35).

Casseroles: If the recipe calls for bread cubes, cashews, ripe olives, or cheese cubes, save out some to make a pattern atop the mixture, such as an initial or dinner bell design. Always garnish casseroles with parsley or water cress.

Fish or Sea Food: Lemon is fish's favorite partner. Make a shamrock of a lemon slice; remove half the pulp from a slice and curl the rind underneath, or make a lemon twist: cut a lemon slice half-way through and twist so it stands up.

Happy Birthday

"Happy Birthday to you," sing family and friends as the candle-lit cake is carried in and another birthday celebration reaches its climax.

These pages include plans for birthday parties for both children and grown-ups. And each birthday party includes a special birthday cake.

Children's birthday parties—in fact, children's parties of all sorts—are most successful if carefully planned according to the age, abilities, and interests of the young guests.

General Suggestions: Many mothers like to invite as many children as the host has years: four guests for Bobby's fourth birthday party. Clear the party room of unnecessary (and breakable) items for as much game space as possible. Have another grown-up or an older brother or sister assist you at the party.

For Children 4 to 6 Years Old: Plan a late afternoon party with young guests ready to go home after a light early supper. They have lots of energy, so plan running and marching games. Alternate active games with quiet ones. Because the interest span of the young is short, games should be changed frequently and explanations kept brief. Since this age loves animals and the circus, we use *My Pet* and *Under the Big Top* as our themes.

For Children 7 to 9 Years Old: Plan an after-school party on *the* day and invite a mixed group, or just boys or girls—as you prefer. At this age, children play to win as individuals and delight in taking dares and challenges. They're imaginative and enjoy making things. They love loot, so have plenty of favors and prizes. Again close the party with a simple supper. The *Cinderella, Faraway Places,* and *Play Ball* parties are for 7 to 9's.

For Children 10 to 13 Years Old: Separate parties are best for this age group. They're great doers, so let them do the decorating, fix costumes, even prepare the food. They're goers, too, and love to go swimming, skating, or for a hayride. Plan games of skill and physical dexterity. A theme for the party aids decorating and planning. The *Space Age* and *Holiday in Hawaii* parties are for 10 to 13's.

My Pet Party

for boys and girls 4 to 6 years old

At this age children begin to take a real interest in pets—both friendly family pets and exotic, imaginary pets they'd like to have.

WHAT TO DO?

Nut Hunt for Kittens and Puppies: Hide about 30 unshelled walnuts or pecans about the room. Divide children into two teams—the kittens and the puppies. Have them practice mewing and barking. At the signal, they start hunting for the nuts. But instead of picking up a nut, they must stand by it mewing or barking until mother or the other grown-up helping with the party comes to put it in the team bag. The team finding the most nuts wins.

Modeling Pets in Clay: Give each child a lump of colored clay and watch the fanciful animals emerge.

Pet Story: For a quiet time before refreshments, mother can read a pet story.

Long-time Favorite Games: Play Drop the Hanky, Farmer in the Dell, London Bridge, and Hide the Thimble.

FLUFFY KITTEN INVITATIONS

Use a folded piece of colored paper for the invitation. On the outside paste 2 fluffy cotton powder puffs, a small one above a medium-sized one—children can help with this. Add kitten's ears and tail with colored pencil. Write the message inside.

PARTY TABLE

Center the table with Puppy Dog Cake (opposite) or arrange several little stuffed animal pets. If rabbits are a popular neighborhood pet, the Bunny Cake (p. 82) might be used as the birthday and party cake.

A print fabric showing pets such as kittens or bunnies would make a fun tablecloth, too.

Children will enjoy the meal much more if seated at small-size tables on small chairs. If you don't have enough you may be able to borrow some.

Balloons: Fun colored balloons, in animal shapes if available, are a must for birthday parties. And balloons can double as place cards at the table or as extra favors.

BOX LUNCH AFTER THE PARTY

**Peanut Butter Sandwiches and
Meat Sandwiches (cut in 1" strips)
Deviled Egg Halves (p. 93)
Carrot and Celery Sticks
(wrapped in colored foil)
Ice Cream
(in covered cardboard cups)
Puppy Dog Cake
(serve after boxes are empty)**

Children will be intrigued with supper in little ribbon-tied boxes. And mother can have them ready in the refrigerator ahead of time.

PUPPY DOG CAKE

Pictured on page 33.

Using Betty Crocker White, Yellow, or Devils Food Cake Mix, bake the batter in an 8" sq. pan and an 8" round layer pan. Pour batter to the same level in both pans for uniform height. Bake as directed; remove from pans and cool.

Cut body, paw, and collar from sq. cake and head, tail, and ear from round cake as shown. Arrange cake pieces on a tray (see sketch, p. 32). Prepare 1 pkg. Betty Crocker Fluffy White Frosting Mix. Frost entire dog, joining all parts. Melt 2 sq. semi-sweet chocolate (2 oz.). Using small spatula, spread chocolate over frosting on ears and collar. Draw eyes and mouth with melted chocolate. Outline body parts with pieces of black licorice (see sketch, p. 32). Give him a big, fat gumdrop nose.

You may want to decorate the Puppy Dog Cake to resemble your family dog. For example, use Betty Crocker Caramel Fudge Frosting Mix and toasted coconut for a taffy-colored cocker spaniel.

Big Top Supper

for boys and girls 4 to 6 years old

Hot Dogs with "the Works"
Baked Beans in Circus Pot
Carnival Angel Cake
or
Carnival Cupcakes
Pink Lemonade   Milk

CARNIVAL ANGEL CAKE

Bake a Betty Crocker Angel Food Cake. When thoroughly cold remove from pan. Prepare Betty Crocker Fluffy White Frosting Mix and frost cake. Dip 4 animal crackers in melted semi-sweet chocolate. With knife, mark top and sides of cake into 8 equal wedges. Sprinkle confetti nonpareil candies over alternate wedges. Put candy in folded waxed paper and tap paper gently to sprinkle candy evenly. Insert colored birthday candles into 4 large gumdrops. Place on white wedges close to center hole. Rest front feet of frosted animal crackers on gumdrops and back feet on frosting.

BIG TOP TABLE

Spread the party table with a cloth of wide red and white stripes, just like the stripes on the circus tent. Center the table with the Carnival Angel Cake.

If you have any novelty serving dishes with elephant or other circus shapes, use them for serving the baked beans. We used a gay carousel cooky jar. Bright-colored ceramic cooky jars in novelty designs will find many uses at children's parties, holding everything from popcorn to potato chips.

CARNIVAL CUPCAKES

Bake cupcakes following directions on Betty Crocker Cake Mix pkg. Frost with Betty Crocker Fluffy White Frosting. Sprinkle with confetti nonpareil candies and top each cupcake with a chocolate-coated elephant from a box of animal crackers.

ELEPHANT INVITATIONS

First copy the outline of an elephant from any circus book or from the apron outline opposite. Then, using gray Manila paper folded in half, let the children cut out the elephant shape. Color the ears with pink crayon. Write the invitation inside, and mail in a white envelope.

WHAT TO DO?

Circus Picture Puzzles: Have these ready for children to start work on the minute they arrive.

Cut pictures of elephants, lions, and tigers from magazines or an inexpensive circus book. Paste on heavier paper, cut in eight pieces, and seal in envelopes. Little guests choose an envelope and complete the picture puzzle. The game can be continued by trading pictures.

Peanut Relay: Use the elephant's favorite food for an active game.

Each child, in turn, reaches into a bag of peanuts-in-the-shell, lifting out as many peanuts as possible on the back of his hand. He must then walk briskly to the goal line carrying the peanuts. Have prizes of a few peanuts wrapped in Pliofilm for all.

ELEPHANT APRON

This is for the birthday child to wear when greeting his guests at the door.

You'll need:
  ½ yard dark gray fabric
  yellow twill tape
  assorted bias tapes and rick-
     racks from sewing basket

Cut fabric 25x17″ and fold lengthwise. Cut elephant shape using right hand half of sketch below as guide. Bind all edges with gray bias tape. Cut two 11″ lengths of twill tape for neck ties, two 17″ lengths for side ties; sew on. Outline elephant's head with white bias tape; outline tusks with colored tape—pink for a girl, blue for a boy. Complete decorations as shown with colored rickracks and decorative tapes.

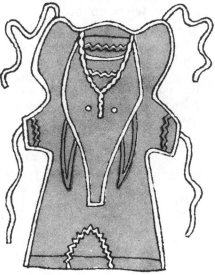

Cinderella Party

for girls 7 to 9 years old

Little girls have always been intrigued with the magical story of Cinderella and they'll love a birthday party planned around a Cinderella theme.

CINDERELLA INVITATIONS

Let the young hostess make her own invitations. Well ahead of the party supply her with an inexpensive Cinderella book, construction paper, and crayons. She can draw (or trace) and color the Cinderella characters for the outside of the invitation; inside she can write "Carolyn's Cinderella Party," date, time, etc.

WHAT TO DO?

Ball Gown Style Show: Young ladies adore dressing up in mother's discarded party dresses in prints and gay colors. Search the attic for flowers, purses, and shoes. Let them promenade through the room as mother describes each outfit.

You are invited to a

THE PARTY TABLE

Cinderella or Fairyland Tablecloth: A few weeks before the party, shop at your fabric department for an inexpensive novelty fabric featuring Cinderella characters or fairyland scenes.

Then, using half a yard of the novelty fabric, cut out figures and appliqué them (by hand or machine) onto a percale tablecloth cut to fit the party table.

Later, the cloth can be used for the special children's table for holiday dinners. And other mothers may want to borrow it for their youngsters' parties.

Real Pumpkin Chariot: If available, a real pumpkin could be transformed into a chariot for the table centerpiece. Place the pumpkin on any four-wheeled toy. Cut out windows and trim them with tiny fabric curtains. Toy horses from a farmyard set could pull the chariot.

FAVORS

At the end of the party give each guest an inexpensive Cinderella story book.

SUPPER WITH CINDERELLA

Princess Sandwiches
Fairy Godmother Fruit Salad
Magic Pumpkin Cake
Royal Palace Punch   **Milk**

MAGIC PUMPKIN CAKE

Pictured on page 33.

Bake Betty Crocker Orange Chiffon Cake Mix in 10″ tube pan. Make Betty Crocker Fluffy White Frosting Mix as directed on pkg. Remove ¼ cup and tint green with about 5 drops of food coloring for stem. Tint remaining frosting with ¼ tsp. *each* red and yellow food coloring to make pumpkin color.

Place cake top-side-up on plate. Frost top, sides, and down inside center hole about 1″ with ¼″ of icing. Spread remaining icing on upper half of sides and outer half of top and shape round like a pumpkin. Make grooves by pulling tip of spatula through frosting, starting at bottom and bringing up to center. For the stem, insert a peeled banana in hole of cake and spread with green frosting. Serve as soon as possible.

ROYAL PALACE PUNCH

Serve one of the delicious frozen fruit punches such as strawberry-lemon punch, diluted with water or ginger ale.

PRINCESS SANDWICHES

As dainty and feminine as Cinderella herself are finger sandwiches of thinly sliced chicken on lightly buttered dark and light bread.

FAIRY GODMOTHER FRUIT SALAD

Combine pineapple tidbits, banana slices, and mandarin orange sections with sweetened whipped cream. Serve on lettuce

Faraway Places Party

for boys and girls 7 to 9

GLOBE INVITATIONS

Cut circles of paper to resemble the globe. Indicate different countries in crayon. Letter in: "Come to my Faraway Places Birthday Party," date, time, place, etc.

WHAT TO DO?

Life in Faraway Places: Give each guest the name of a faraway country. Each in turn describes life in that country as compared to life in America. Give a prize for the best description.

Age of Exploration: Obtain one of the large chronological charts of the Age of Exploration. Pin it up on the wall and allow guests to look it over carefully. Then make a game of calling out famous dates of exploration, like 1492, and answering with the name of the explorer and the place explored.

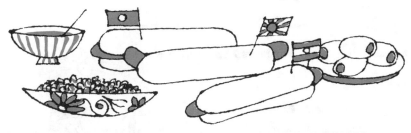

SUPPER FOR SAILORS AND SAILOR-ETTES

Round-the-World Hot Dogs
Seven Seas Fruit Cup
Sailboat Cake
Sea Foam Sipper

ROUND-THE-WORLD HOT DOGS

Serve lots of broiled wieners on hot buttered toasted buns. To give the wieners a Round-the-World air, serve relishes that come from many places. Explain that the sliced stuffed olives come from Italy, the heated pineapple spears from Hawaii, the mustard from China, the hot chili sauce from Mexico, and so on.

SEA FOAM SIPPER

Serve tall glasses of cold Strawberry or Raspberry Milk topped with whipped cream "sea foam."

STRAWBERRY OR RASPBERRY MILK

cold milk
raspberry or strawberry jam or
**   ice cream topping or thawed**
**   frozen berries**
red food coloring

For each serving, beat or shake 1 cup milk with 2 heaping tsp. jam, topping, or berries. Add 2 or 3 drops coloring, if desired.

ANCHOR CUPCAKES

Serve these and save the sailboat cake for a family party later, if you like.

Using a pastry tube or an envelope with a tiny corner cut off, frost a chocolate anchor on each white-frosted cupcake. Leave cupcakes in paper cups for easy handling.

SAILBOAT CAKE

Pictured on page 33.

Using your favorite Betty Crocker Cake Mix, bake ½ the batter in 9" sq. pan and ½ in 8 or 9" round layer.

Cut cooled 9" sq. cake as shown (p. 32). Note that A is slightly larger than B. Arrange cake pieces on tray as shown. Prepare 1 pkg. Betty Crocker Creamy White Frosting Mix. Put ⅓ of frosting in another bowl and tint red; then put another ⅓ in bowl and tint light blue. Frost sail in horizontal red and white stripes, frost hull of boat blue. *Or frost sail white and hull brown (⅔ frosting plus 3 tbsp. cocoa). Add hard candies for portholes on the hull. Place birthday candles in gum–drop holders in a row on cake tray.

Sports Party

for boys 7 to 9 years old

PLAY BALL PARTY

The famous sports writer, Grant-land Rice, once said, "For when the One Great Scorer comes to write against your name, He marks —not that you won or lost—but how you played the game."

Playing the game, whether it's base-ball, football, or basketball occupies much of the leisure time of boys from this age on up. So why not plan his birthday party around a ball game theme?

WHAT TO DO?

Take the boys to see a game.

Or arrange for the boys to play their own game. During the winter, a basketball hoop may be put up in the basement. Even shooting the ball into a big wastebasket is competitive and good exercise. For a safer game for younger boys, use the light plastic "fun" balls and bats.

Borrow from the public library a film or movie of a famous game.

PARTY TABLE

The Baseball Mitt Cake or the Football Field Cake surrounded with candles, is all the centerpiece or table decoration you'll need.

FAVORS

Give an inexpensive book on sports, sportsmanship, or a famous player.

As a special remembrance for your son, have a new ball for all the guests to autograph, just as the big league players autograph balls for souvenirs.

YEA, TEAM! SUPPER

**Fried Chicken
Scalloped Potatoes
Hot Buttered Green Vegetable
Giant Relish Tray
Pennant Ice Cream
Baseball Mitt Cake with Baseballs
or Football Field Cake**

FOOTBALL FIELD CAKE

Heat oven to 350° (mod.). Make batter using Betty Crocker White, Yellow, or Devils Food Cake Mix. Spread batter in greased and floured jelly roll pan, 15½x10½x1". Bake *20 to 22 min.* Turn out of pan onto large tray or bread board covered with aluminum foil; cool.

Frost top and sides with Betty Crocker Chocolate Fudge Flavor Frosting Mix. Make a little decorator icing by thinning confectioners' sugar with milk or cream. With decorating tube, make yard and goal lines; outline football field and fill in. Make goal posts with wooden skewers or lollipop sticks; make crossbars on goal posts with drinking straws fastened with cellophane tape.

Baseball Field or Basketball Court: Make cake as above—*except* decorate as baseball field or basketball court.

SCALLOPED POTATOES

These are so easy with pre-packaged Betty Crocker Scalloped Potatoes.

BASEBALL MITT CAKE

with Baseball Cupcakes

Pictured on page 33.

Prepare batter using Betty Crocker Yellow Cake Mix. Bake in greased and floured jelly roll pan, 15½x10½x1", *20 to 22 min.* Cool in pan 10 min. Remove and finish cooling.

Baseball Mitt: Place right hand on left side of cake and trace around it. Enlarge size of fingers and extend to make mitt about 9½" from fingers to wrist. Cut around outline. Hollow palm of mitt slightly. Frost with Betty Crocker Caramel Fudge Frosting Mix. Cut licorice rope candy into short strips and lay between fingers for laces.

Baseballs: From remaining cake, cut baseballs using 2 to 2½" round cutter. Frost tops and sides with Betty Crocker Creamy White Frosting Mix. Fill decorating tube with remainder of frosting used on mitt. Draw stitching lines on baseball as shown. Place one ball in palm of mitt. Put birthday candles in the other balls and arrange around the mitt.

PENNANT ICE CREAM

Slice pint bricks of Neapolitan ice cream so that each slice has a stripe of chocolate, vanilla, and strawberry.

Space Age Adventure Party

for boys 10 to 13 years old

An afternoon of adventuring in outer space is sure to capture the imaginations of the young rocket scientists in your neighborhood.

INVITATIONS

A sample ticket for a trip to outer space opens up to reveal party details.

SOLAR SYSTEM TABLECLOTH

Get a large inexpensive map of the solar system and outer space. Cover the table with a plain-colored cloth, then lay out the map. Cover the map with transparent plastic if you wish to preserve it.

Boys will enjoy looking at the solar system map before you serve the birthday supper.

WHAT TO DO?

Orbiting the Moon: All sit in a circle. One guest who knows the game starts. He says, "I'm going to orbit the moon and I'm going to take . . ." (here he names an article of clothing). To be correct he must name something worn by the person on his left. After he names the article the next person repeats the phrase and he, too, names an article. If he doesn't name something worn by the person on his left, he cannot orbit the moon this round. Go around the circle until every one has caught on to the trick.

Radar Search: Choose an "Explorer" and send him out of the room. While he is gone, hide an object somewhere in the room. When the "Explorer" returns, the group seated in a circle on the floor imitates a radar set. As the "Explorer" moves closer to the object the group makes a loud "Blip, Blip" noise. As he moves away they "Blip" softly. When the "Explorer" finds the object, he chooses a new "Explorer."

SUPPER AFTER SPACE AGE FUN

Sputnik Cheeseburgers
Satellite Tomatoes
Rocket Cake
Saturn Sodas

SPUTNIK CHEESEBURGERS

Prepare open-face cheeseburgers. Garnish with pickle slices held in place with colored toothpicks.

SATELLITE TOMATOES

Cut small carrots, celery sticks, and green onions the same length, about 3½". Wash med. tomatoes; peel, if desired. To make satellites, remove tomato cores. Make two small slashes about ½" long in each tomato on either side of hole where core was removed. Insert a carrot stick and a celery stick. Insert onion in center of each tomato. Serve as individual salads.

SATURN SODAS

Since yellow-orange rings surround Saturn, serve a scoop of orange sherbet in each tall glass of cold orange-flavored soft drink.

ROCKET CAKE

Bake Angel Cake Roll as directed on Betty Crocker Angel Food Cake Mix pkg. Fill with Cocoa Fluff (below) and roll along long edge into 15" roll. Prepare Betty Crocker Creamy White Frosting Mix, tinting a small amount red in a separate bowl. Frost roll, decorating with a 1 to 2" wide red band around the middle. Finish with a shiny nose cone fashioned of heavy-duty aluminum foil. Add tail fins at back (use sugar wafers or 5" right triangles of white cardboard).

Cocoa Fluff: Mix 1 cup whipping cream, ½ cup *sifted* confectioners' sugar, ¼ cup cocoa, and a dash of salt in chilled bowl. Beat until stiff enough to hold point.

FAVORS

Give books on planets and space travel selected according to the children's reading levels.

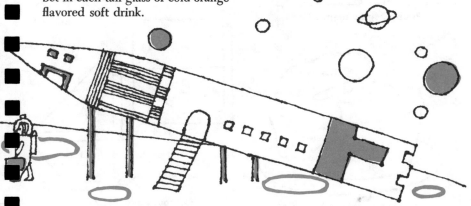

FUN CAKES

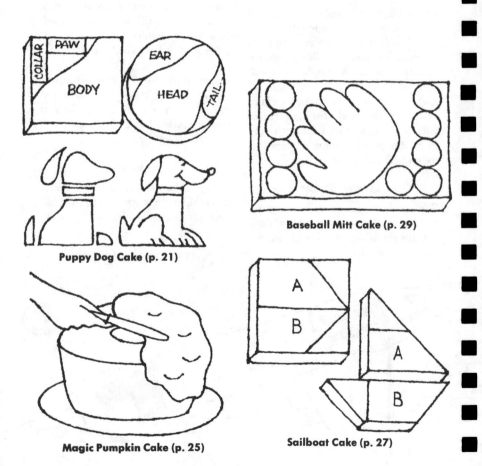

Baseball Mitt Cake (p. 29)

Puppy Dog Cake (p. 21)

Magic Pumpkin Cake (p. 25)

Sailboat Cake (p. 27)

USE PINK AS A THEME FOR TEA FOR MOTHER'S DAY

Use as much pink as you wish in table decorations and refreshments.

Pink Net Party Cloth: This is perfect for a wedding reception too. Select pink nylon net for the floor-length ruffle and a pale pink wash-and-wear fabric to cover the table top and to make under-skirt for ruffle. Measure table edge and buy 1½ to 2 times length of net so that ruffle will be full.

Sew a loose gathering stitch 1″ from top of ruffle, gather to fit, then sew to straight piece of fabric. To cover table: spread pink fabric on table allowing an inch or two overhang, then simply pin the ruffle to cloth at edge of table.

This cloth fits any size or shape table as ruffle is pinned to fit. Top cloth is flat for easy laundering.

Pink and Violet Centerpiece: Top a white glass cake stand with bunches of violets tied with pink net . . . centered with pink rose and violet corsage.

Holiday in Hawaii Party

for girls 10 to 13 years old

ALOHA INVITATIONS

The young hostess may enjoy making her own invitations. Cut and fold yellow construction paper to fit standard 5x3" envelopes. On the outside, letter *Aloha*, using a different color for each letter. Inside, write the invitation. (*Aloha* means greetings, with love, or farewell.)

WHAT TO DO?

Hula Language Lesson: Girls will love to learn more about the hula, the famous dance of our island-state. Find someone who knows the hula hand language. (Mother may want to study it herself.) Play soft Hawaiian-style music in the background, seat the girls in a circle, and teach this graceful hand language.

"Aloha" and Its Story: Teach them the melodic "Aloha Oe" and tell them the story of the brave Queen Liluokalani.

HAWAIIAN HOSPITALITY

Greet guests at the door with gaily colored paper leis and flowers to wear. Serve a cold fruit punch in coconut cups (cut fresh coconuts in half or cut top ⅓ from coconut, as shown on p. 35).

FAVORS

Paper leis are the party favors. Cut or buy 1½" wide strips of pretty colored crepe paper. Using a large needle and double string or thread the length of expected lei, gather paper strip through the center lengthwise. Draw gathers up tightly, fasten ends, and twist into spiral.

ISLAND ATMOSPHERE

Trim room with Hawaiian travel posters. Cover low tables (card tables placed flat on the floor or coffee tables) with fern leaves. Guests sit cross-legged around tables. Center the table with a punch bowl of water with flowers and flower-candles floating in it.

HAWAIIAN SUNSET SUPPER

Pictured on pages 34-35.

Cold Fruit Punch in Coconut Halves
Luau Pork Sandwiches
Sweet Potato Casserole
Salad Tropicale
Coconut Palm Cake

LUAU PORK SANDWICHES

Favorite food of the native feast, or *luau*, is the pig which has baked all day in a pit.

Just as festive is well-seasoned barbecued pork (wonderful use for leftover pork roast) served on toasted buns or bread.

SALAD TROPICALE

Bananas, pineapple, and citrus fruits are a must in a fruit salad for a Hawaiian party. Add melon balls or other fruits according to the season. Serve in dessert dishes or in one of the following special ways:

Melon Bowl for Salad: Fruit salad becomes a conversation piece when served in a hollowed-out watermelon half.

Fruit-filled Pineapple Boats: Cut fresh pineapple in half, leaves and all. Cut out core and fruit leaving shell about ½" thick. Serve each guest a pineapple boat filled with Salad Tropicale.

COCONUT PALM CAKE

Bake Betty Crocker White, Yellow or Devils Food Cake Mix in 8" layer pans. When cool, fill and frost with Betty Crocker Fluffy White Frosting Mix. Sprinkle sides of cake thickly with shredded fresh coconut (1½ to 2 cups). On top of cake arrange a coconut palm tree using a cinnamon stick or chocolate candy roll as a trunk, with slices of green peppermint gumdrops as leaves, and chocolate pieces as coconuts. Place birthday candles in holders around cake.

To Prepare Fresh Coconut: Pierce 3 holes at one end. Drain milk. Heat in mod. oven (350°) *30 min.* Cool. Break shell with hammer or chisel; remove. Break meat in pieces. Pare off brown skin. Grate or shred white meat. If tops cut from coconuts are to be used, heat cut-side-down to prevent drying.

Italian-Style Supper Party

for teen agers

Although teen agers may not want a full-scale birthday party, they will enjoy inviting the gang to supper before the game or dance.

ITALIAN-STYLE SUPPER

**Old Country Italian Spaghetti
Tossed Green Salad
Salty Bread Sticks
Cheeses   Fresh Fruit
Spumoni Cake**

SPUMONI CAKE

Bake Betty Crocker Devils Food Cake Mix in layers. Slice horizontally into 4 layers. Whip 2 cups whipping cream with ½ cup *sifted* confectioners' sugar until it forms soft peaks. Divide into 4 parts. Put cake together with Fillings (right). Wrap aluminum foil around sides of cake and chill or freeze until serving time. If frozen, thaw 2 to 3 hr. before serving. *12 servings.*

Green Pistachio Filling (bottom layer): To ¼ of the whipped cream, add: 4 to 6 drops green food coloring, ½ tsp. vanilla, ¼ cup chopped pistachio nuts.

Pink Peppermint Filling (second layer): To ¼ of the whipped cream, add: 4 to 6 drops red food coloring and ¼ cup crushed peppermint candy (about 3 sticks).

Golden Rum-flavored Filling (third layer): To ¼ of the whipped cream, add: 4 to 6 drops yellow food coloring and ½ to 1 tsp. rum flavoring.

Spicy Cocoa Fluff Topping: To remaining whipped cream, add: ¼ tsp. cinnamon and 3 tbsp. *sifted* cocoa.

To frost cake completely with whipped cream, whip an additional cup of whipping cream with ¼ cup *sifted* confectioners' sugar and add ½ tsp. cinnamon and 3 tbsp. *sifted* cocoa.

OLD COUNTRY ITALIAN SPAGHETTI

For Meat Balls

¼ cup olive oil
1½ lb. ground beef
¼ lb. ground pork
1 cup fine dry bread crumbs
1 clove garlic, cut fine
½ cup milk
½ cup grated Parmesan cheese
½ onion, chopped (about ⅓ cup)
1 egg, beaten
1 tbsp. minced parsley
½ tsp. salt
¼ tsp. pepper
⅛ tsp. *each* cinnamon, allspice, nutmeg
¼ tsp. lemon juice
⅛ tsp. *each* basil, oregano, red pepper

For Sauce

two no. 2 cans tomatoes
6-oz. can tomato paste
1 cup water
1 tsp. basil
⅛ tsp. *each* basil, oregano, red pepper
1½ tsp. salt
¼ tsp. black pepper

two 7-oz. boxes spaghetti or 1 lb.

PASTA CENTERPIECE

The various forms of pasta—spaghetti, noodles, shells, rigatoni—make an interesting centerpiece for a buffet table. A trip to an Italian grocery store will reveal dozens of these unusual shapes, ranging from tiny bowknots to large sea shell forms, which can be bought in small amounts and arranged in a colorful bowl.

Heat olive oil in large heavy kettle. Form meat and remaining meat ball ingredients into balls 1 to 2" in diameter. Brown balls, half of them at a time, in oil.

Remove meat balls from kettle and add sauce ingredients. Cook uncovered over med. heat about 1 hr., stirring occasionally. Add meat balls, cover and cook an additional 20 min. Just before sauce is done, cook spaghetti. Top with meat balls and sauce. Pass grated Parmesan cheese. *6 to 8 servings.*

A Party for Adults

FOR GROWN-UPS

Though elaborate birthday parties are seldom given "after 21," grown-ups nonetheless enjoy observing *their* day with friends and family.

Here's an extra-special chocolate cake that will fit into all your birthday party plans, whether it's dessert after an evening at the theater or served at an impromptu gathering of neighbors.

CHOCOLATE BUTTER-MALLOW CAKE

⅓ cup soft shortening
1 cup sugar
½ cup brown sugar (packed)
2 eggs (½ to ⅔ cup)
1 tsp. vanilla
2 sq. unsweetened chocolate
  (2 oz.), melted
1¾ cups *sifted* SOFTASILK
  Cake Flour
1½ tsp. soda
¾ tsp. salt
1 cup buttermilk
¼ cup water

Heat oven to 350° (mod.). Grease and flour an oblong pan, 13x9⅜x2". Combine shortening, sugars, eggs, vanilla, and cooled chocolate. Cream until fluffy (beat 5 min. high speed on mixer or by hand). Sift together flour, soda, and salt. Add alternately in 3 additions with buttermilk. (Start and end with dry ingredients.) Finally, blend in water. Pour into pre-

pared pan. Bake *35 to 40 min.*, until toothpick stuck in center of cake comes out clean. Let stand 10 min. Remove from pan. Cool. Finish with Butterscotch Filling and Marshmallow Frosting.

Butterscotch Filling

1 cup brown sugar (packed)
3 tbsp. flour
1 cup milk
2 egg yolks, slightly beaten
2 tbsp. butter
1 tsp. vanilla
½ cup chopped nuts

Combine sugar and flour in saucepan. Gradually stir in milk. Cook over med. heat, stirring constantly, until mixture thickens and boils. Boil 1 min., stirring constantly; remove from heat. Slowly stir at least half of hot mixture into egg yolks. Blend into remaining hot mixture in saucepan. Boil 1 min. more, stirring constantly. Remove from heat and blend in butter and vanilla. Cool. Spread on top of cake to within ½" of edge, and sprinkle with nuts.

Marshmallow Frosting

2 egg whites*
1½ cups sugar
¼ tsp. cream of tartar
1 tbsp. light corn syrup
⅓ cup water
¼ lb. marshmallows, quartered
   (about 16 whole)
½ sq. unsweetened chocolate
   (½ oz.), melted

Combine egg whites, sugar, cream of tartar, syrup, and water in top of double boiler. Place over boiling water and beat with electric or rotary beater until mixture stands in stiff peaks. Scrape pan occasionally. Remove from heat; add marshmallows. Continue beating until frosting is thick enough to spread. Frost cake. Drizzle melted chocolate in rows the length of cake. Then draw knife through frosting across rows for wavy effect.

* See copyright page

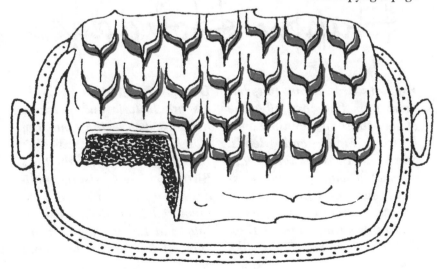

Happy Holidays

Holidays are always fun, but more than that they offer the chance to strengthen the bonds between family and friends. Some of these holidays are associated with religious occasions, such as Christmas and Easter. Some are family days, as Mother's Day, Father's Day, and Thanksgiving. Some, like Halloween and St. Valentine's Day, are for children. Still others are historic and patriotic holidays such as the Fourth of July, Memorial Day, Lincoln's Birthday, and Washington's Birthday. The Christmas holidays and summer picnics on Memorial Day, the Fourth of July, and Labor Day offer enjoyment for the whole family and all of their friends.

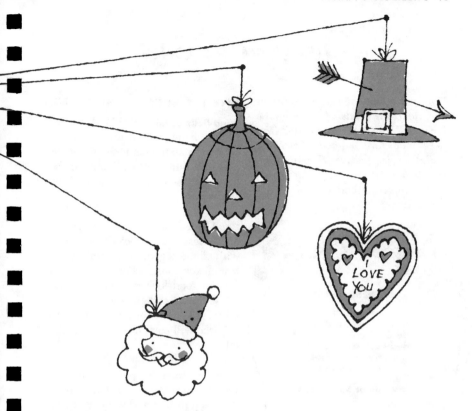

It doesn't matter what the occasion is, it's always nicer when there is a festive air, when food and decorations have been worked out together. In this section we have collected food ideas and hints for decorations appropriate to each holiday. In some instances you may be inspired to adapt some of these ideas for other special occasions—such as a dinner party before a dance, or a tea for a special and dear friend.

In any case, we hope that this section will help you to enjoy your entertaining more, to increase your reputation as a hostess, and to make your holidays happier the year 'round.

New Year's Eve Buffet

Why not adapt the colorful customs and delicious foods of the Chinese for your New Year's Eve party? Chinese foods are a good choice for buffet service because they are bite-size (they were originally eaten with chopsticks and thus don't require knives).

CHINESE FEAST

Egg Roll
Shrimp-filled Mushrooms
Pineapple Chicken   Beef Curry
Fried Pork with Walnuts
Fluffy White Rice
Chinese Cabbage
Fresh Fruit   Almond Cookie
Jasmine or Spiced Tea

Ahead of Time: Bake cookies; completely cook chicken and curry, and refrigerate; fill mushrooms.

If Time is Short: Buy frozen beef, pork, or shrimp chow mein, fried rice, and eggs foo yung. Heat and serve chow mein from a handsome chafing dish. Serve chilled mandarin oranges and fortune cookies for dessert.

GIVE THE HOUSE A CHINESE AIR

Wind-Bells at Midnight: With a wide ribbon, hang a set of those wonderful hand-painted Chinese wind-bells over the buffet table. They can be jingled at the midnight hour on New Year's Eve.

Good Luck Table: Use a bright yellow or Chinese red tablecloth decorated with Chinese good luck symbols cut from black construction paper. Look for the good luck symbol in a book on Chinese calligraphy at the library. A Chinese-inspired floral centerpiece will complete your Oriental table.

Why not dress the part? As hostess for a Chinese party you may want to go a step further and wear the traditional straight-cut Chinese dress with high collar, short sleeves, and side-slit skirt. Inexpensive ones are available in the Chinatown sections of large cities, or make one. Use the dress for other at-home hostessing later.

INVITATIONS

If you send written invitations you can paint the Chinese good luck symbol in red and black on simple folded notes to give your guests a hint of what's in store.

PINEAPPLE CHICKEN

1 lb. chicken breasts
cornstarch
dash of pepper
cooking (salad) oil
1 tbsp. salt
soy sauce
8 slices canned pineapple (cut in
 wedges) or 13½-oz can pineapple tidbits (1⅔ cups)
1 clove garlic, minced

BEEF CURRY

1½ tbsp. cooking (salad) oil
1 med. Spanish onion, sliced in
 rings
2 to 3 tsp. curry powder
1½ lb. lean flank steak, cut
 in 1" cubes
½ lb. fresh mushrooms, sliced
1 tomato, diced
1 large clove garlic, minced
2 tsp. salt
2 tsp. sugar
2 tbsp. cornstarch
2 tbsp. water

Heat oil in heavy skillet. Sauté onion over med. heat, just until tender. Stir in curry powder; cook 1 min. Add beef cubes and remaining ingredients in order listed. Continue cooking until beef cubes are lightly browned. Add enough boiling water to barely cover beef (about 2 cups). Cover skillet and simmer gently *about 1½ hr.* or until beef is extremely tender. Thicken with cornstarch-water mixture. Serve with steamed rice. *4 to 6 servings.*

Remove skin from uncooked chicken breasts and cut them into ¼" slices. Remove meat clinging to bone with kitchen shears. Add mixture of 2 tsp. cornstarch, pepper, 2 tbsp. cooking (salad) oil, salt, and 2 tsp. soy sauce to meat. Drain pineapple and save juice. Heat 1 tbsp. cooking (salad) oil in skillet and fry chicken until just underdone. Add pineapple, cover skillet, and cook chicken and pineapple together 3 min. In a smaller skillet, heat 1 tbsp. cooking (salad) oil and fry the minced garlic. Add mixture of 3 to 4 tsp. soy sauce, ¼ cup water, ½ cup pineapple juice, and 4 tsp. cornstarch; stir until thickened. Place chicken and pineapple on platter and cover with brown sauce. Garnish with parsley. *4 servings.*

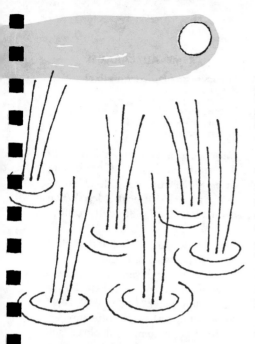

FRIED PORK WITH WALNUTS

1½ lb. pork tenderloin
2 tbsp. soy sauce
1 tbsp. brown sugar
3 tbsp. flour
5 tbsp. cooking (salad) oil
1 cup shelled walnut halves
1 tbsp. soy sauce

Cut pork into 1½ x ½″ pieces. Toss in mixture of 2 tbsp. soy sauce, brown sugar, and flour. Heat 3 tbsp. of the oil in large skillet over low flame, until oil is hot. Add pork a little at a time. Cook covered until pork is brown and tender, about *30 min.* Remove pork. Place 2 tbsp. oil in skillet and sauté walnuts over low heat until brown and crispy. Add pork and sprinkle 1 tbsp. soy sauce over top, stirring lightly. Heat pork and walnuts about *5 min. 4 servings.*

SHRIMP-FILLED MUSHROOMS

1 lb. mushrooms (large caps)
two 4½-oz. cans shrimp, finely chopped
½ cup minced celery (about 2 stalks)
½ lb. very lean pork, finely ground
½ tsp. salt
dash of pepper
⅓ cup cooking (salad) oil
2 tbsp. soy sauce
1 cup chicken broth

Wash mushrooms and remove stems. Mix shrimp, celery, pork, salt, and pepper. Pile mixture generously into mushroom caps. Heat oil, soy sauce, and chicken broth in large heavy skillet over med. heat, or use electric fry pan. Place mushrooms in skillet, filled-side-up. Cover and cook *30 min.,* until pork is thoroughly done.

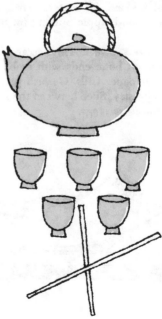

NEW YEAR'S DAY DINNER

Clear Consommé
Crown Roast of Pork
Petit Potatoes with Onions
Julienne Green Beans
Tomato Aspic Cubes
over Tossed Greens
Hard Rolls
Crème au Caramel

CROWN ROAST OF PORK

Have crown made at meat market from two strips of pork loin containing about 20 ribs (6 to 8 lb.). (For easy carving, have backbone removed.) Season with salt and pepper. Place in roasting pan, bone ends up; wrap bone ends in aluminum foil to prevent excessive browning. Roast uncovered in slow oven (325°), *20 to 25 min. per lb.* of meat, 2 to 3 hr. An hour before meat is done, fill center with 2 qt. Orange and Apple Stuffing (p. 51).

To Serve Crown Roast: Replace foil wraps on bone ends with crab apples or paper frills. Garnish platter with parsley. Slice between the ribs. *About 20 servings.*

CREME AU CARAMEL

½ cup sugar (to caramelize)
3 eggs
⅓ cup sugar
¼ tsp. salt
2 cups milk, scalded
½ tsp. vanilla

Caramelize ½ cup sugar. Pour into 6 custard cups or a 1½-qt. baking dish. Move cups or dish about so that caramel will coat sides. When caramel is hard, fill with custard.

Heat oven to 350° (mod.). Beat eggs, sugar, and salt slighty to mix. Stir in milk and vanilla. Pour into caramel-lined cups or dish. Set in pan of hot water (1″ deep). Bake *45 to 50 min.*, just until knife inserted 1″ from edge comes out clean (soft center sets as it stands). Unmold; melted caramel runs down sides forming a sauce.

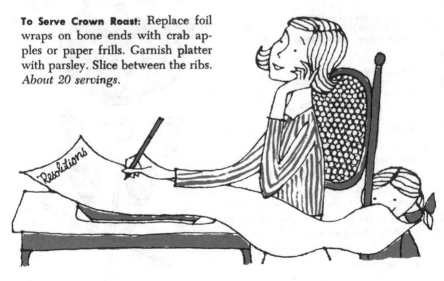

You may wish to substitute a traditional holiday food, Roast Suckling Pig, in the place of the roast pork on the opposite page. Be sure to consult your meat dealer early, as this specialty is not always available. Plan suckling pig for a large elegant party—though costly, it will be a meal to remember.

ROAST SUCKLING PIG

15 to 18-lb. suckling pig
2 tsp. salt
½ tsp. freshly ground
   black pepper
dash of garlic powder
Orange and Apple Stuffing
   (recipe right)
¼ cup butter, melted
2¾ cups boiling water
fruit for garnish

Wash pig in cold water and wipe dry. Combine salt, pepper, and garlic. Rub into inside of pig. Stuff loosely with stuffing. Close opening of pig's body cavity with skewers and lacings. Wipe the outside of the skin and rub with melted butter. Place a small block of wood in pig's mouth to brace it for the apple to be inserted later. Place pig, in kneeling position, on a rack in a large shallow pan. Pour boiling water in pan and cover with foil. Remove foil 1 hr. before roasting time is up so that the pig may get brown. Roast in 325° oven *about 4 hr.*, until tender, basting every 45 min. with water in pan. Add more water if necessary. *10 to 12 servings.*

Orange and Apple Stuffing: Prepare 4 qt. Bread Stuffing (p. 112). Add 2 cups chopped apple, 2 cups diced orange or mandarin orange sections, and 4 tsp. grated orange rind.

To Garnish Pig: Place pig on a large serving platter. Place small red apple in mouth. Insert maraschino cherry in each eye socket. Place a garland of cranberries around pig's neck.

To Carve Suckling Pig: Cut through skin around neck and along sides. Peel off skin and, with knife, scrape off layer of fat just below skin. Then cut pig along spine, cracking the tender backbone. Next, cut off legs at hip bone joint. Then cut ribs, two for each diner. Cut some meat from ham and shoulder for each serving. Head meat is a delicacy.

Lincoln's Birthday

Because Lincoln spent his early years in a log cabin, simplicity and homespun charm are the keynotes in entertaining on his birthday. As a young man, our great Civil War president kept store and split logs by day, and read law by the firelight in the evening.

COUNTRY-STYLE SUPPER

Oven Barbecued Beef
Boiled Potatoes   **Green Beans**
Corn Bread
Fresh Spinach and Onion Ring Salad
Apple Brown Betty

DECORATING YOUR TABLE

Why not set the table as it might have been in Lincoln's day? Use a red-and-white or blue-and-white checked tablecloth with dark blue or red napkins of paper or a simple cotton. Set the table with white china and dark blue or red tumblers, if you have them.

Arrange shiny red apples in a wooden chopping or salad bowl, tucking pine sprays in here and there for your table centerpiece.

For a real Early American atmosphere, have white candles in hurricane lanterns to light the dining table.

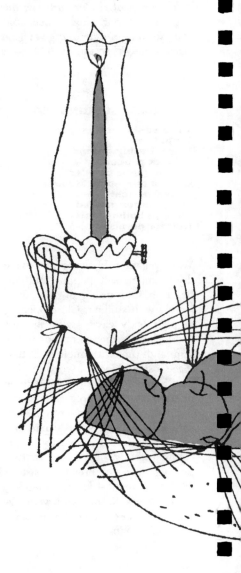

ESPECIALLY FOR LINCOLN'S BIRTHDAY

Since Lincoln was a rail splitter, and logs have become his symbol, here are a few suggestions for serving food.

Lincoln Log Dessert: Make a chocolate-frosted chocolate cake roll.

Brownie Logettes: Draw prongs of fork lengthwise in chocolate frosting to resemble bark.

Log-shaped meat loaves and yeast rolls.

Snack Log: Use any small smooth log, such as birch (birch logs are often sold at Christmastime for use as candleholders). Make small holes in it by pounding a nail in here and there. In each hole, insert a colored toothpick with a simple hors d'oeuvre on the end (an olive, cube of cheese or ham, shrimp, etc.).

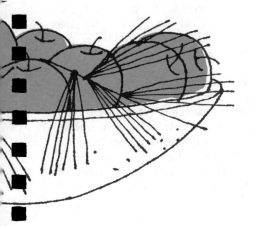

OVEN BARBECUED BEEF

3 lb. round steak (¾″ thick)
2 tbsp. cooking (salad) oil
½ cup chopped onions
¾ cup catsup
½ cup vinegar
¾ cup water
1 tbsp. brown sugar
1 tbsp. prepared mustard
1 tbsp. Worcestershire sauce
½ tsp. salt
⅛ tsp. black pepper

Heat oven to 350° (mod.). Cut steak into 10 equal portions. Pour oil into skillet. Brown each piece of steak on both sides. Transfer steaks to roasting pan. Add onions to oil in skillet and brown lightly. Add rest of ingredients to make a barbecue sauce and simmer in skillet 5 min. Pour sauce over steaks in pan. Cover. Bake *2 hr.*, until meat is fork tender. *6 to 8 servings.*

Valentine's Day

This mid-February day has been a festival of romance since the days of ancient Rome, when Juno and Pan were feted. After the coming of Christianity, the holiday was named in honor of Bishop Valentine.

A VALENTINE BUFFET SUPPER

Lobster Newburg
in
Heart Croustades
Baked Canadian Ham
Buttered Peas with Mushrooms
Pink Grapefruit-Avocado Salad
Hot Rolls
Heart-shaped White Coconut Cake

HEART CROUSTADES

Heat oven to 375° (quick mod.). Slice bread 2" thick. Remove crusts; cut into heart shapes. Cut out center, leaving ¼" thick wall on bottom and sides. Brush with melted butter. Bake until golden, *12 to 15 min.*

HEART-SHAPED WHITE COCONUT CAKE

Bake Betty Crocker White Cake Mix batter in two 8" heart-shaped pans. When cool, put together with a lemon filling. Frost with Betty Crocker Fluffy White Frosting. Sprinkle top and sides of cake thickly with shredded coconut.

DECORATING YOUR TABLE

If you own a beautiful lace tablecloth, this Valentine buffet dinner party is the time to bring it out. Use lace or cut work mats for the smaller dining (card) tables or put them on individual trays.

For a larger, more formal party, you may want to use a floor length cloth with a flounce of ruffled net (p. 37) for the buffet table. A washable pink floral design fabric could be used for cloths on the card tables for dining. Pin matching bows of the same floral fabric to corners of the buffet table.

ESPECIALLY FOR VALENTINE'S DAY

How to Serve Your Food: Serve heart-shaped foods and red and pink food to say, "Be my valentine." Your favorite sugar cookies cut in heart shapes and decorated with silver shot, cinnamon hearts, or gumdrops are a treat for the children. Heart-shaped sandwiches are festive at a tea or lunch. And for dessert, try filling baked heart-shaped meringue shells with strawberries and ice cream.

Use heart-shaped molds for aspic or red fruit molded salads. Serve food on pretty lacy doilies garnished with hearts.

HEART TART SHELLS

Heat oven to 475° (very hot). Make pastry for two-crust pie. Divide into 6 equal parts. Place one piece of pastry on a 7″ sq. of foil, cover with a 7″ sq. of waxed paper, and roll into circle to edges of paper. Remove waxed paper. Using paper pattern, cut out a heart of foil and pastry with scissors. Shape the two into a heart-shaped tart, turning up edge about 1″ and fluting it. Repeat with remaining pastry. Bake *8 to 10 min.* on baking sheet. Cool; fill as desired. Foil may be removed before serving. *6 tarts.* Use this method for fancy tarts of all sorts.

HAM ROLL-UPS

Heat oven to 350° (mod.). Roll ¼ cup Curried Rice (below) in each of 12 slices boneless ham or sliced boiled ham. Secure with wooden picks. Place in baking dish and cover with foil. Bake *15 to 20 min.*

Curried Rice: Sauté 1 tbsp. minced onion in 2 tbsp. butter until yellow. Stir in 3 cups boiled white rice, ¼ tsp. salt, ¼ tsp. pepper, and 1 tsp. curry powder.

ANGEL CAKE ROLL

Bake an Angel Cake Roll following directions on Betty Crocker Angel Food Cake Mix pkg. Spread cooled roll with 1 qt. softened strawberry ice cream. Roll as directed.

PINK ALASKA PIE

Bake 8″ pie shell, tinting pastry pink before rolling it out.

Soften 1 qt. strawberry ice cream. Pile into cooled baked pie shell and freeze overnight.

Heat oven to 500° (very hot). Make pie meringue by beating 3 egg whites with ¼ tsp. cream of tartar until frothy, then gradually beating in 6 tbsp. sugar. Add ½ tsp. flavoring. Tint a delicate pink. Arrange peaches on ice cream. Spread meringue over pie, covering entire surface and sealing edges. Bake on a wooden bread board *about 5 min.* until lightly browned. Serve at once.

EASY-CREAMY SHRIMP

Place contents of 10-oz. can frozen cream of shrimp soup in saucepan; add ½ cup milk. Heat slowly; stir often, until sauce reaches boiling point and is smooth. Add 4½-oz. can broken shrimp, drained, or whole little Italian shrimp. Heat 5 more min. Serve over fluffy white rice tossed with chopped pimiento.

HEART COFFEE CAKE

**2 cans Betty Crocker Bisquick
    Refrigerated Biscuits
¼ cup butter, melted
¾ cup sugar
1 tbsp. cinnamon (3 tsp.)
¼ cup chopped nuts**

Heat oven to 375° (quick mod.). Grease an 8″ heart-shaped cake pan. Separate biscuits and dip in melted butter; coat entirely with mixture of sugar and cinnamon. Place 15 to 16 biscuits around outer edge of pan, overlapping to fill. Overlap remaining 4 to 5 biscuits in center to fill pan. Pour remaining butter over top. (There will be a very small amount left.) Sprinkle with nuts. Bake *25 to 30 min.* Allow to stand 5 min. before serving. Turn out coffee ring on rack, then over again on serving plate, with the nut side up. *About 10 servings.*

HEART CUT-OUT SANDWICHES

Using small square (pullman) loaves, cut a small heart from center of half the slices with cooky cutter. Butter bread and spread whole slices with ham salad or tomato-cheese filling. When put together, pink filling shows through heart.

WITH LOVE TO YOUR FAMILY ON VALENTINE'S DAY

Valentine's Day is a good time to show your family how much they mean to you by making a colorful valentine tablecloth.

The cloth sketched below is bleached muslin bordered with red cotton and edged with inexpensive braid, also red.

In the center of the cloth, work out a design of hearts with birds and flowers cut from colored fabric remnants, both plain and print; appliqué these in place by hand or machine. Complete the design with letters TO MY VALENTINES, also cut from fabric and stitched on. You may want to follow the design shown or take your inspiration from any Pennsylvania Dutch design.

For a simpler cloth, cut as many red fabric hearts as you have children. Embroider their names on the hearts and sew on a white or pink cloth.

Children can make original tablecloths, too. Let them draw and color hearts, birds, and flowers on a white cloth or place mats. Then make their drawings permanent and washable by ironing them on the wrong side.

VALENTINE PARTY

for girls 8 to 12 years old

AFTERNOON REFRESHMENTS
Valentine Cupcakes
Salted Nuts
Strawberry Milk (p. 27)

VALENTINE SUPPER

Creamed Chicken
in
Pimiento Mashed Potato Nests

Celery Hearts   Radish Roses
Ice Cream
Milk

VALENTINE CUPCAKES

Bake cupcakes using your favorite Betty Crocker Cake Mix. Frost with Fluffy White Frosting. Decorate top of each cupcake with heart design piped on with red Easy-creamy Icing (p. 83). Cover cupcake sides with pink-tinted shredded coconut.

To Tint Coconut: Add food coloring to water. Let coconut soak in it until desired color. Drain; dry.

PARTY-PRETTY TABLE

Cover the table with the special Valentine cloth (p. 57), or use a red cloth with paper lace place mats.

Tree of Hearts: Make a table-size holiday tree as described on p. 79. Trim with red paper hearts of many sizes *or* fancily decorated heart-shaped cookies *or* heart candies. Tuck tiny artificial flowers or a few artificial birds here and there as you wish.

WHAT TO DO?

Children are happier, and so are you, if they are engaged in a constructive activity.

Valentine-decorated Cooky Boxes: Have mother make lots of simply decorated heart-shaped cookies (p. 126). Get a variety of clean empty food containers, red paper, lace paper doilies, magazines and seed catalogs from which to cut flowers, ribbon, paste or glue, paints, and brushes. Each guest can use imagination and artistic ability in covering and decorating cooky containers. The little girls will be delighted to take decorated boxes full of cookies home to their families, to shut-in friends, or to a "room" party at school.

Some specific directions for covering boxes are on the opposite page.

VALENTINE DECORATED COOKY BOXES

Rolled Oats or Corn Meal Box: Cover with red adhesive-backed paper (cut paper the height of box and length of circumference). Decorate with cut out paper flowers. Add a row of bias tape, lace edging, or ribbon at top just below lid. Trim lid with paper doily and more flowers.

Cake Mix Box: Turn an empty cake mix pkg. into a Valentine house. Make a roof by folding a piece of construction paper. Hold roof in place with ribbon pulled through slits in roof and around box. Decorate with a door and windows.

Tea Box: This is for tiny cookies. Cover with pink paper and decorate with bows of rose-colored pipe cleaners and white bias tape.

Washington's Birthday

Because Washington was born to a life of luxury, we associate colonial elegance with entertaining on his birthday. General Washington and his charming wife, Martha, loved nothing better than entertaining friends at Mount Vernon, their beautiful plantation home.

A supper party menu typical of those served in Virginia in colonial times included: curried shrimp on rice, roast chicken, scalloped corn, hot biscuits, Sally Lunn (a fluffy yeast bread baked in a tube pan), plum preserves, peach pickles, tossed green salad with melon balls, floating island, and pound cake.

FOR BOUQUET BEAUTY

Fresh Green Leaves: For the look of fresh flowers without the price, use artificial flowers with fresh green leaves. For Washington's birthday, combine a few gold leaves with fresh greens and red carnations, real or artificial.

Lemon, huckleberry, or fern from the florist will mingle with your plastic or paper flowers and make them come to life. The few sprays of leaves you'll need will cost very little. Put the greens in a glass of water nestled among your artificial flower stems.

Silver or Gold Leaves: Even children can color leaves with silver or gold paint. First cover the floor with newspaper. Use any large leaves on slender branches. Paint fronts and backs of leaves. (It isn't necessary to cover them *completely.*) For a faster job, try a spray. Leaves will last as long as a month.

FEBRUARY 22nd FAMILY SUPPER

Little Ham Loaves with Cherry Sauce
Scalloped Corn
Tossed Green Salad
Hot Biscuits
Floating Island   Pound Cake

LITTLE HAM LOAVES WITH CHERRY SAUCE

1⅓ lb. smoked ham
⅔ lb. fresh pork
2 eggs
soft bread crumbs (2 slices bread)
¾ cup milk
1 tbsp. granulated sugar
½ tsp. *each* cloves and cinnamon
dash of pepper
¼ cup brown sugar (packed)
1 tbsp. prepared mustard
1¼ tsp. milk

Heat oven to 350° (mod.). Grind ham and pork together. Mix in eggs, crumbs, ¾ cup milk, granulated sugar, cloves, cinnamon, and pepper.

Shape into 6 individual log-shaped loaves. Place in greased pan. Combine brown sugar, mustard, and 1¼ tsp. milk; spread over loaves. Bake 1¼ hr. Serve hot with Cherry Sauce (heated canned cherry pie filling). *6 servings.*

ESPECIALLY FOR WASHINGTON'S BIRTHDAY

Legend says Washington chopped down the cherry tree, and ever since cherries and hatchets have been symbols of George Washington. Why not show them in your food?

Cherry-decorated cakes and cookies
Chocolate-covered cherries
Cherry-centered ice cubes
**Cherry sauce to serve over ice cream
 or warm cake**
Pastry hatchet cut-outs on cherry pie
Hatchet-shaped biscuits and cookies

St. Patrick's Day

And did you know St. Patrick wasn't Irish? Pirates brought him to Ireland as a lad of 16. He later escaped, returned to England, and became a monk. A vision led him back to Ireland where, as a missionary, he converted thousands to Christianity.

Legend says he planted the shamrock, Ireland's national flower.

EMERALD ISLE BUFFET

Corned Beef Hash, Buffet Style
Shredded Cabbage-Apple Salad
Shamrock Biscuits
Lemon Ice with Mint Sauce
Green-iced Angel Food Cake

CORNED BEEF HASH, BUFFET STYLE

Heat oven to 400° (mod. hot). Combine three 1-lb. cans of corned beef hash and ½ cup chopped onion. Place corned beef mixture in baking dish, 11½x7½x1½". Pour ½ cup cream over hash. Bake 35 min. Remove from oven and arrange 16 deviled egg halves on hash. Serve with heated chili sauce or catsup in Pepper Pot. 8 to 10 servings.

Pepper Pot: Cut green pepper as shown. Stem becomes handle of lid. Scoop out seeds. Fill with heated chili sauce or catsup.

ARRANGE YOUR VEGETABLES

Vegetables, with their beautiful shapes and colors can make an attractive centerpiece for St. Patrick's Day.

Arrange green vegetables in a low container, applying the same design principles you follow in arranging flowers. Let a few of the vegetables extend over the side of the dish for a more natural look. A bunch of celery cut flat on the bottom to stand up will add height. If you wish, place a few wooden copies of the famous Irish white clay pipes among the vegetables.

ESPECIALLY FOR ST. PATRICK'S DAY

Spark your meals with Irish green.

Green pineapple rings for salads or broiled with meat.

Greens in abundance, especially parsley and water cress.

Guacamole dip (avocado mashed with onion and lemon juice) for chips or as a spread for bread.

Green ices and ice creams—such as pistachio, lime, and mint.

Green frostings for cakes and cookies; green cream cheese frosting for a sandwich loaf. For delicate tints, add food coloring with a light hand.

Shamrock shapes for cookies, biscuits, etc. are easy with a "club" cutter.

Green shamrock candies to garnish individual fruit cocktails, butter, frosting, or cookies.

Easter

Easter is a day of joy commemorating Jesus Christ's resurrection from the dead. Worship services in flower-decked churches with magnificent music mark the day. But even before the Christian era, there were springtime festivals marking the end of winter and the return of new life to the earth. The egg as a symbol of new life has become an emblem of Easter.

Easter traditions in America include the visit of the Easter bunny, New York's famous Easter Parade, and the "egg rolling" at the White House.

EASTER EGGS

Pictured on pages 70-71.

Empty egg shells are best to use because they need not be refrigerated as hard-cooked eggs must be, and favorite fancy ones can be kept from year to year.

Prick a hole in both ends of a fresh egg with a needle. Blow egg from shell. If blowing is difficult, enlarge hole with needle. (Refrigerate egg yolk and white immediately for scrambled eggs.) Wash egg shell and dry; decorate.

Mark egg into geometric sections as the Ukrainians do their elaborately designed eggs.

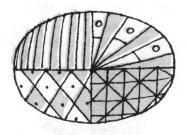

With pencil, divide the egg in half lengthwise; then across the center. Divide each section in half again for a geometric pattern to follow in putting on decorations.

Apply bits of adhesive tape to eggs before dyeing. When removed, a white pattern appears (see blue egg, p. 71). Or wind rubber band around eggs before dyeing (see green egg at bottom of p. 70).

Rickrack and bias tape glued on in geometric patterns make unique eggs. Green and pink are pretty Easter colors.

Sequins, flowers, and ribbons from craft departments are easy to use and fun to attach. Try tiny artificial flowers with rows of ribbons and little matching bows.

Beads and buttons make decorations with imagination. Try rhinestone buttons with rows of gold tape and pink velvet ribbon. (Use white glue.)

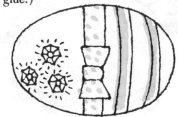

MORE EASTER EGG IDEAS

Egg Heads: Paint faces on empty egg shells. Make hair and/or hats with paper lace doilies, yarn, scraps of fabric, anything at hand. Set upright on collar a 1″ wide strip of cardboard slit and made into a ring.

Egg 'n Chick: Cut top off colored empty egg shell leaving zigzag edge. Fill egg with paper grass. Top grass with fluffy yellow paper chick from variety store.

Piglets: Start with brightly colored eggs. Add paper tail and ears, a nose and four short legs of gumdrops.

Easter Egg Carton: Cover a cardboard egg carton with purple paper. Stuff each egg space with paper grass as a cushion for twelve of your prettiest decorated eggs.

JEWEL GELATIN EASTER EGGS

Break shells of 8 or 9 eggs so carefully that just the tip of the shell is broken when egg is removed. Wash and dry shells. Dissolve 1 pkg. lemon-flavored gelatin in 1 cup boiling water and *only* ½ cup cold water. Divide gelatin mixture into 3 bowls; tint ⅓ green and ⅓ red with food coloring. Arrange empty shells upright in egg carton or egg shelf from refrigerator and fill with colored gelatin. Chill until firm.

To remove eggs from shells: carefully break away shell about halfway, hold egg under warm running water a moment, and invert to slip egg out. Serve as dessert in nests of green coconut or as salad in nests of greens.

CHOCOLATE FUDGE EASTER EGGS

Make Chocolate Fudge as directed on pkg. of Betty Crocker Chocolate Fudge Flavor Frosting Mix—*except* (using a funnel) pour fudge mixture slowly into hole in one end of Empty Egg Shells (p. 64). Seal hole at lower end with tape. Let stand a minute to make sure egg shell is full. Seal hole at top of shell. Place in refrigerator to harden. When chilled, peel off shell. Decorate with white or pastel-tinted Easy-creamy Icing (p. 83).

MACAROON EASTER EGGS

Mix Betty Crocker Coconut Macaroon Mix as directed on pkg. Tint part of dough, if desired. Chill 15 min. Heat oven to 350° (mod.). Dust fingers with confectioners' sugar and mold teaspoonfuls of dough into egg shapes. Place on paper-covered baking sheet and bake *about 12 min.*, until peaks are lightly browned. Cool. Melt 4 sq. semi-sweet chocolate (4 oz.) (enough to coat half the eggs). Hold eggs on fork and dip in chocolate. Chill about 1 hr. until coating is firm. Decorate the plain eggs with frosting, if desired. *Makes 3 doz.*

FONDANT EASTER EGGS

**1 pkg. Betty Crocker Creamy
      White Frosting Mix
5 tbsp. soft butter
3 tbsp. flour
2 tbsp. hot water**

Combine frosting mix, butter, and flour; add hot water. Knead 20 to 30 times on a board lightly dusted with confectioners' sugar. Divide into 3 parts tinting each a pastel color with food coloring. Shape into eggs of various sizes using ½ to 1½ tbsp. fondant each. Chill. Decorate chilled eggs with colored Easy-creamy Icing (p. 83) or Decorator Icing (p. 68) piped on with rosette tip.

Or coat eggs with chocolate prepared according to directions on pkg. of dipping chocolate.

EASTER BASKET CAKE

Bake Betty Crocker Orange Chiffon Cake in 10″ tube pan. Decorate cake as basket. Fill basket with green-tinted coconut "grass" and candy Easter eggs from the variety store or Fondant Eggs (p. 67).

To Make Basket: Shape a nest for eggs by using a sharp knife to cut a sloping slice from edge to center of cake. Cut center no deeper than ½″. Fill hole made by tube pan with cut cake.

To Frost Basket: Tint Betty Crocker Fluffy White Frosting Mix pale yellow. Frost sides of cake and lightly frost top. Make a basket weave pattern in frosting on sides of cake by drawing inch-long horizontal and vertical lines with tines of fork. Cover top of basket with green-tinted coconut.

For Basket Handle: Fashion handle of pipe cleaners or coat hanger. Wrap several strips with aluminum foil. Then wrap handle with pastel yellow ribbon; make ribbon secure with cellophane tape. Tie mauve ribbon on top. Press handle into top of cake basket.

NOTE: *To tint coconut:* add green food coloring to water. Let coconut soak in it until desired color. Drain; dry.

71

Easter Eggs (see pages 64-65)

FANCY FISH NET TABLECLOTH AND DEEP SEA CENTERPIECE

Less than an hour's work will turn a humble fish net into a fancy tablecloth sure to please a fisherman-father. Save the cloth for other fish dinner parties.

First, shop for a fish net to fit your table. Mail order houses offer inexpensive nets as small as 6x4'.

Next, decorate the net. Outline fish and waves using white and aqua rug yarn as shown. Tie or embroider them on, using more of the same colored yarn. "Water bubbles" are curtain rings tied on. Add luminous green buttons for fish eyes. Some nets come complete with rope edges and wooden bobbers at corners. If net is not finished, add corks at corners as anchors.

Cover table with blue or green cloth, then lay on net.

Arrange centerpiece of a conch shell holding sea fans and sea grape leaves; add a starfish on either side. Be sure to use any fish-shaped serving pieces you may have.

If you can't find these deep-sea specialties at your florist's, try a display supply store. A telephone directory will provide the names of such stores. Or write your nearest one for a catalog listing many fascinating accessories which will give all your parties a decorative flair.

EASTER SUNDAY BREAKFAST

Bouquet Cocktail
Scrambled Eggs with Avocado Balls
Pan-fried Canadian Bacon
Orange Muffins
Orange Marmalade
in Grapefruit Basket

BOUQUET COCKTAIL

Tape lace paper doily around top of sherbet glass to look like the frill on an old-fashioned bouquet. Fold 6 to 8″ doily in fourths, cut out small arc in center, and experiment with glass for size. Fill glass with fruit, such as pineapple chunks with halved (lengthwise) fresh strawberries. Garnish with mint or water cress.

SCRAMBLED EGGS WITH AVOCADO BALLS

Heap hot scrambled eggs on warmed platter. Top with avocado balls; garnish with water cress or parsley.

To Make Avocado Balls: Press flat side of ball cutter or ½ tsp. measuring spoon into peeled avocado. Keep turning until ball is formed.

FESTIVE WAYS TO SERVE FOOD

A Pretty Bread Basket: Entwine any artificial flowers around handle. Line basket with paper doily; tuck more flowers into holes in doily here and there.

A Grapefruit Basket for Marmalade: Remove sections and juice from a grapefruit half; wash. Make pliable handle (p. 86) of pastel satin ribbon faced with wire; press ends into grapefruit edge. Tie real or artificial spring flowers to top of handle with bow. Fill basket with marmalade, jelly, or jam.

Plate-in-a-Nest: For any Easter meal, set plate in a wreath of green paper grass.

More Scrambled Egg Ideas: During last minutes of cooking, add one of these: grated Cheddar cheese, crisp bacon bits, sautéed mushrooms, or finely chopped ham.

HOT CROSS BUNS

1 cup warm water (not hot—110
   to 115°)
1 pkg. active dry yeast
2 tbsp. sugar
2¼ cups *sifted* GOLD MEDAL Flour
1 tsp. salt
1 tsp. cinnamon
¼ tsp. nutmeg
1 egg
2 tbsp. soft shortening
½ cup currants
¼ cup chopped citron

In mixing bowl, dissolve yeast in water. Stir in sugar, half the flour, salt, and spices. Beat with spoon until smooth. Add egg and shortening. Beat in rest of flour, currants, and citron. Scrape down sides of bowl and cover with a cloth. Let rise in warm place (85°) until double in bulk, about 30 min.

Grease 12 large muffin cups. Stir down raised dough. Spoon into muffin cups filling ½ full. Let rise in warm place until dough reaches tops of muffin cups, 20 to 30 min. *Heat oven to 400° (mod. hot).* Bake *15 to 20 min.,* until brown. Make a cross on each bun with Easy-creamy Icing (p. 83). *Makes 12 buns.*

HONEY BUNNY BISCUITS

Heat oven to 450° (hot). Remove biscuits from 1 can Betty Crocker Bisquick Refrigerated Biscuits. Place 5 biscuits on ungreased baking sheet.

Cut remaining biscuits in half; lengthen halves to form ears.

Press ears to whole biscuit to form bunny head. Press in raisin eyes, candied cherry nose, and slivered almond whiskers. Bake *8 to 10 min.,* until golden brown. Frost ears with Easy-creamy Icing (p. 83) tinted pink. *Makes 5.*

TRADITIONAL HAM DINNER

**Baked Ham with Orange Glaze
and Bunny Garnish
Twice-baked Potatoes
Spinach with Rosemary
Hot Rolls
Strawberry-Rhubarb Mold
Easter Daffodil Cake**

STRAWBERRY-RHUBARB MOLD

**2 cups rhubarb sauce (16-oz. pkg.
frozen sweetened rhubarb,
cooked as directed or made
from fresh rhubarb)
1 pkg. strawberry-flavored
gelatin
9-oz. can crushed pineapple**

Make rhubarb sauce; heat to boiling. Remove from heat and immediately add gelatin to hot sauce and stir until dissolved. Cool until partially set. Add drained pineapple, reserving 2 tbsp. for dressing. Pour into 1-qt. ring mold. Chill until firm. Serve on crisp greens with:

Crushed Pineapple Dressing: Combine ¼ cup whipping cream, whipped, ¼ cup mayonnaise, and the reserved crushed pineapple.

EASTER DAFFODIL CAKE

Bake Betty Crocker Lemon Custard Angel Food Cake Mix. Cool. Frost top and sides of cake with cooled vanilla pudding (cooked-type mix). Sprinkle toasted coconut over top and sides. Chill. When ready to serve, arrange three daffodils with lemon leaves in center hole of cake. Arrange more lemon leaves around base.

BUNNY GARNISH

Children enjoy Easter festivities so much, why not trim your ham with a young outlook? This bunny garnish of fruit takes only a few extra minutes.

On a sheet of waxed paper, arrange a large peach half for the bunny's body. Use a smaller peach half (cut one down if necessary) for the head. Cut two more peach halves as shown for legs and arms. Finish with marshmallow-half ears, clove eyes, licorice whiskers, and a carrot.

Surround bunny with a garland. Use marzipan, the tiny flower-and-fruit-shaped candies sold in department and candy stores. Or alternate colored filled candies with tiny parsley bouquets.

After ham comes from the oven, let it cool about 20 min. for easy carving. Then quickly put on the bunny, all ready on waxed paper. Surround ham with lemon leaves or leaf lettuce and peach and pear halves, cut-side-down.

ORANGE GLAZE

Spread mixture of ½ cup orange marmalade and 2 tbsp. honey over scored baked ham the last 40 min. of baking.

IN-A-HURRY HAM DINNER

**Cranberry-glazed Broiled Ham Slice
Mashed Potatoes
Buttered Asparagus Spears
Tossed Green Salad
Brown 'n' Serve Rolls
Pineapple Ice
Easter Brownies (p. 83)**

CRANBERRY-GLAZED BROILED HAM SLICE

Split fat around edge of 1" thick precooked ham slice. Trim off excess. Broil 5 min., 3" from heat. Turn. Broil 3 min. Then spread thinly with prepared mustard and whole cranberry sauce. Broil 3 min. more.

ESPECIALLY FOR EASTER

**Round yeast rolls baked in a pie pan and frosted to look like a nest of pastel-tinted eggs
Colorful bonnets fashioned of cookies and cake
Bunny cookies and cakes with flaked coconut "fur"
Chicken-shaped cookies and sandwiches**

BUNNY TABLE RUNNER
FOR EASTER

This is the first in a series of easy-to-make holiday runners. Place it over your plain-colored tablecloths to dress them up for party meals.

We suggest a purple percale or drip-dry runner with white terry cloth bunnies appliquéd on it. The soft, fuzzy terry cloth makes wonderful bunnies. You can copy them from the drawing above or from a child's coloring or story book.

Appliqué baskets of flowers on either side. With a little imagination and a pretty spring flower cotton print you can make many patterns. We made the flower baskets of purple rickrack and tulip-printed percale. The runner was finished with harmonizing stripes of bias tape.

This runner could be made in any pastel color. It would be delightful for a young child's birthday party. And don't be surprised if other mothers want to borrow it.

You may wish to protect the runner with a sheet of lightweight clear plastic when you use it.

A matching apron for Mother may be made of the same flowered print used for flowers on runner. Make a basket-shaped pocket outlined in bias tape. (For child's bunny apron, see p. 81.)

"HAPPY HOLIDAY" TREE

A tree that can be trimmed according to the holiday or occasion is a helpful accessory for the successful party-giver.

Gather medium-sized tree branches to stand in a pot or bucket of sand on the floor to brighten a hall or corner. Or arrange smaller branches in a flowerpot or vase for use on a table. Spray branches with white or metallic paint if you wish.

With careful storage, branches can be used for parties for several years.

Enchanting Easter Tree: Trim tree with one or more of the following: Easter cookies, artificial spring flowers, chocolate marshmallow bunnies, colored plastic-foam eggs, or beautiful imported small novelty candies. Bank the base with green paper grass.

PERSONALIZED EASTER EGGS

Surround the roast chicken or turkey with nests of water cress, parsley, or green paper grass. In each one, place a colored Easter egg with the name of a person at the table on it.

DINNER ON EASTER SUNDAY

Chilled Cranberry Cocktail
Roast Chicken or Turkey with Stuffing
Mashed Potatoes   Creamy Gravy
Buttered Peas with Cauliflowerets
Molded Garden Salad Tray
Pineapple-Strawberry Parfaits
Easter Cookies

Cut up bread and celery for stuffing the day before; stuff bird just before roasting. Make molded salads a day ahead; finish the tray an hour before serving and refrigerate.

MOLDED GARDEN SALAD TRAY

Garden Salad: Prepare 1 pkg. lemon-flavored gelatin, adding 2 tbsp. lemon juice. Chill and, when partially set, add ¼ cup finely sliced green onions, ½ cup diced cucumber, ½ cup *each* thinly sliced radishes and celery, and 1 tsp. salt. Pour into 6 individual molds. Chill.

Tray: Unmold salads on greens on tray or chop plate with bowl of mayonnaise in center. Fill spaces on tray with ripe and green olives, pickled crab apples, and peaches.

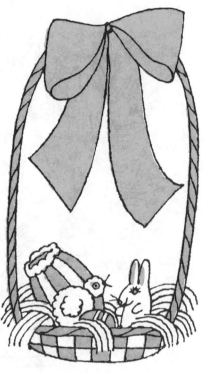

PINEAPPLE-STRAWBERRY PARFAITS

1 pkg. Betty Crocker Coconut Macaroon Mix
2 cups commercial sour cream
2 tbsp. brown sugar
2 cups cubed-sweetened fresh or canned pineapple (about 1 med. pineapple)
1 cup sliced, drained, sweetened strawberries

Prepare Macaroons as directed on pkg. Cool. Finely crumble 10 macaroons into bowl; blend in sour cream and sugar. Cover and chill 2 to 3 hr. To serve: layer chilled fruits and sour cream mixture in parfait glasses or dessert dishes; serve immediately. *6 to 8 servings.*

BUNNY APRON

Give it as a prize or let the young host or hostess wear it to welcome the guests.

Cut a triangle of white terry cloth 27x18x18" for body. Cut 8" circle of white terry for head. Cut 13x3" strips of pink terry for ears. Sew together.

Work buttonhole on one ear, sew button on the other. Ears button around neck.

Instead of attaching ties, make a cotton tail (coil of white brush fringe) and loop of tape to fasten together at the back.

Finish bunny with black bias tape whiskers, button eyes, and a pink rickrack bow tie.

CHILDREN'S EASTER PARTY

For an afternoon of fun for children 5 to 7 years old, plan an Easter egg hunt; then serve a simple supper.

WHAT TO DO?

Easter Egg Hunt: Hide jelly bean eggs indoors or out. Give the children little baskets or sacks in which to carry the eggs they find. Plan prizes for the ones who gather the most and the least eggs and for the child who finds the Alleluiah Egg.

Alleluiah Egg: Decorate a pink egg with a purple cross and white tulips.

Songs and Games: Play Easter songs such as "Here Comes Peter Cottontail" on the phonograph or piano as children hop or dance. Have a race with children hopping like bunnies for a certain distance.

EARLY SUPPER AFTER THE PARTY

**Mugs of Hot Soup
Deviled Eggs
Bunny-shaped Ham Sandwiches
Peter Rabbit's Favorite Foods
(fresh vegetable relish tray)
Easter Bunny Cake**

The soup mugs may be paper cups decorated with Easter stickers. Drinking soup through straws is fun for children.

Dress up the supper table with the Bunny Table Runner (p. 78). Use paper plates. Cover plates with pastel lace doilies.

EASTER BUNNY CAKE

Bake Betty Crocker White or Yellow Cake Mix in layers according to directions on pkg.

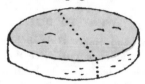

Cut one cooled layer in half. Put halves together with Betty Crocker Fluffy White Frosting Mix or whipped cream.

Stand up on cut edge. Cut out piece to indicate rabbit's head. Use cut-out piece for tail, securing with toothpick.

Frost with remaining icing and cover generously with coconut. Cut ears of folded white paper; color inside pink. Use pink candies for eyes and nose.

Coconut tinted green, or paper grass and a few Easter eggs form an attractive nest for the bunny.

BUNNY-SHAPED SANDWICHES

Cut white bread with bunny cooky cutter. Spread with butter. Fill with sliced ham and lettuce. Add a bit of carrot for bunny's eye. Put slice of carrot in bunny's hand.

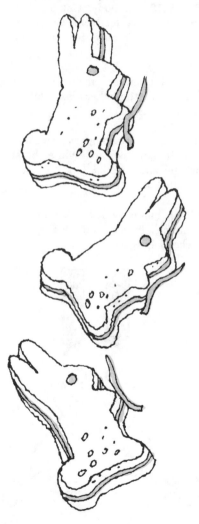

EASTER FINERY FOR COOKIES

Easter Bonnet Cookies: Bake round sugar cookies. Paint complexion with pink-tinted Easy-creamy Icing (right); add eyes, nose, and mouth with blue icing. Fold a small paper doily for the bonnet and attach white strings or ribbons that tie under chin of the cooky face.

Sunflower Girl Cookies: Use little girl-shaped cooky cutter. Make skirt from lace paper doily.

Bunny Cookies: Use bunny-shaped cutter. Trim with pink frosting, white coconut, and raisin eye.

Humpty Dumpty Easter Cookies: Use Humpty Dumpty cutter. Decorate with pastel frosting; add raisin eyes.

Easter Egg Cookies: Make your own "egg" cooky cutter: using an empty frozen juice or soup can with both ends removed, squeeze can into oval shape.

Cut eggs out of Mary's Sugar Cooky dough (p. 126). Bake. Decorate with pastel-tinted icing.

EASTER BROWNIES

Prepare chocolate fudge-frosted brownie squares. Decorate with bunny face. Split a marshmallow: draw a face with toothpick and food coloring on one half; snip other half for ears.

EASY-CREAMY ICING

Blend 1 cup *sifted* confectioners' sugar, ¼ tsp. salt, ½ tsp. vanilla or other flavoring (lemon, almond, etc.), and liquid (about 1 tbsp. water or 1½ tbsp. cream) to make easy-to-spread icing. Tint, if desired, with a few drops of food coloring. Spread with spatula or pastry brush.

May Day

In days gone by, May 1 was the date of a happy festival dedicated to Flora, goddess of flowers and spring. Both a king and a queen of the May were chosen.

Today in America, children make May baskets, fill them with wild flowers, candies, or cookies, and hang them on doorknobs at the homes of friends.

EASY-TO-MAKE MAY BASKETS

Carton Basket: *Start with* empty cottage cheese or pint ice cream carton. *Cover with* colored paper—whatever you have on hand: shelf paper, gift wrap, wall paper, metallic or construction paper. *Finish with* pliable handle made by fastening fine wire to back of satin ribbon with cellophane tape. Place bow on top of handle.

ESPECIALLY FOR MAY DAY

Flower-shaped sandwiches, cookies
Basket-shaped cookies "filled" with little frosting flowers or sugar paste flowers from the variety store
Maypole cake
Meringue baskets (bake handles separately) filled with ice cream and berries

Lacy Basket: *Start with* 8″ circle of dark colored construction paper, 8″ lace paper doily, and cellophane tape. Tape paper and doily together. Make 8 cuts through the 2 thicknesses, ending each cut at edge of doily center. Tape the 8 doily-and-paper sections together at sides. *Form basket* using doily center as base; fold each lace-covered section toward it, one cut edge overlapping the other. Tape into position from inside. *Finish with* pliable handle made by fastening fine wire to back of satin ribbon with cellophane tape.

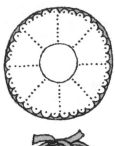

CHICKENBURGERS-IN-A-BASKET

½ lb. Cheddar cheese
2 sweet pickles
2 cups cut-up cooked chicken
1 tsp. grated onion
6 tbsp. mayonnaise
10 hamburger buns

Chop cheese and pickles finely. Add chicken, onion, and mayonnaise. Season to taste. Split and butter buns. Fill with chicken mixture and replace tops. Wrap in aluminum foil and refrigerate. When ready to serve, heat in mod. oven (350°) *15 min. 10 servings.* Serve in a doily-lined basket, with a bunch of flowers tied to the handle.

MAKE-A-MAY-BASKET PARTY

Doing something for others is a wonderful reason for a party for pre-teen girls. Your daughter can invite a group of friends for an afternoon of making and filling May baskets for children in the hospital or for shut-ins. This is a good idea, too, for a May birthday party.

BASKET-OF-FLOWERS CUPCAKES

Frost cupcakes with white or chocolate icing. With decorating tube, make roses, violets, buttercups, and green leaves of icing on top of cakes —or shape flowers and leaves of cut-up colored gumdrops. Ribbon-covered wire handles transform cakes into baskets of flowers.

Chickenburgers-in-a-Basket
Carrot Straws
Basket-of-Flowers Cupcakes
Grape Juice-Ginger Ale Punch
or Hot Cocoa

BOUQUETS FOR EACH GUEST

Cover table with a pastel cloth, with a lace paper doily or mat at each place. For a centerpiece, arrange individual bouquets of spring flowers, real or artificial, in a low bowl or basket—one bouquet for each guest to take home.

Mother's Day

In 1908, Anna Jarvis of Grafton, West Virginia, conceived the idea of Mother's Day. She sent five hundred white carnations, her mother's favorite, to be given to those attending the first celebration. In 1914, President Woodrow Wilson proclaimed Mother's Day a nationwide occasion.

MOTHER, GUEST OF HONOR

Dad and the youngsters can easily manage this do-ahead oven dinner.

*Roast Lamb, Beef, or Pork
Oven-browned Potatoes
Buttered Asparagus with
Nutmeg Butter
Jellied Fruit Salad   Bread Sticks
Decorated Cake
°*Let mother choose her favorite.*

Here's how to do it: Prepare salad ahead of time. Buy a decorated cake at your neighborhood bakery. Roast and potatoes bake while you set the table, wrap mother's gift, and prepare other foods.

MOTHER'S DAY COMES AT LILAC-TIME

A low basket filled with fresh-cut lilacs makes a perfect Mother's Day centerpiece. Trim the basket handle with a bit of pink net and a lavender bow.

GIFT-WRAP TO MATCH YOUR CENTERPIECE

For unusual gift-wraps, cut out paper folders to hold small gifts. Here's how to make a basket gift-wrap:

Cut double basket shape of purple paper. Punch holes at sides and lace with ribbon; or seal edges together with cellophane tape.

Add pliable handle of orchid ribbon strengthened with wire fastened to back with tape.

Fill basket with tissue-wrapped gift of jewelry or perfume. Add a little lilac sprig or two.

MOTHER-AND-DAUGHTER TEA
Pictured on page 36.

Shrimp-Cucumber Rounds
Tiny Tea Puffs **Tea Brownies**
Cherry Thumbprint Macaroons
Salted Nuts **Hot Fruited Tea**
Hot Coffee

HOT FRUITED TEA

5 cups boiling water
5 tea bags or 5 tsp. tea
10 whole cloves
¼ tsp. cinnamon
½ to ¾ cup sugar (depending on sweetness of fruit)
½ cup lemon juice
⅓ cup fresh orange juice
3 orange cartwheel slices

Pour boiling water over tea. Add cloves and cinnamon. Cover and let steep 5 min. Strain tea; add sugar and citrus juices. Heat to just below boiling. Serve hot with half cartwheel slice in each cup. *6 servings.*

SHRIMP-CUCUMBER ROUNDS

Cut thin bread slices into 2″ rounds. Spread lightly with softened cream cheese. Top with a cucumber slice centered with a small shrimp.

TINY TEA PUFFS

Using 1 stick Betty Crocker Cream Puff Mix, prepare 60 bite-size cream puffs using 1 tsp. dough for each. Just before serving, fill with chicken, ham, or sea food salad.

CHERRY THUMBPRINT MACAROONS

Make macaroons as directed on Betty Crocker Coconut Macaroon Mix pkg. Immediately after removing from oven, make thumbprint in each cooky. Fill with candied cherry.

Memorial Day

Memorial Day is set aside to honor fighting men who gave their lives. Called Decoration Day, it was first observed in 1868 to remember the men who fought in the Civil War.

EASY PICNIC—AT HOME OR AWAY

**Grilled Hamburgers on Toasted Buns
Vegetable Shish-kabobs
Potato Chips
Fresh Rhubarb Pie**

VEGETABLE SHISH-KABOBS

**small whole onions
small whole tomatoes
zucchini squash
fresh mushrooms**

Wash all vegetables. Parboil the whole onions 8 to 10 min.; drain and cool. Slice zucchini ½ to ¾" thick. Arrange vegetables in large bowl or platter.

Prepare outdoor grill 45 min. before ready to use. When coals are hot, alternate an onion, a tomato, a zucchini slice, and a mushroom cap on a metal skewer. Brush with melted butter, sprinkle generously with salt and freshly ground pepper. Grill over hot coals, turning often until vegetables are tender. Brush on more butter and sprinkle on more seasoning during cooking. Serve with grated Romano or Parmesan cheese.

VEGETABLE SCARECROW

If you plan a party in the back yard, arrange the vegetables for Shish-kabobs on a large wooden platter, so that when it comes time to skewer, you have everything ready.

On the center of your platter stand a cucumber in a floral frog. Using toothpicks, attach 2 green pea pods for arms, and a sliced cucumber wedge for the head. Carrot curls make the hair and a large mushroom is the cap. Cut red construction paper for lips and black for eyelashes; paste on.

FUN PICNIC ACCESSORIES

Take your party with you. Pack food, plates, grill, and charcoal.

Carry cooked foods safely and serve them with a flair from plastic refrigerator dishes decorated with decals or wallpaper. You can carry out one decorative theme on all your picnic accessories—such as Western, boats, fruit, or floral motifs. For inspiration, flip through some old wallpaper books.

Fresh fruits and vegetables travel well in tin or plastic boxes, again decorated. Take dressing for tossed salad in a gaily designed screw-top glass jar. To make the decoration permanent, shellac.

Special Picnic Cloth: A fabric tablecloth and napkins lend some of the comforts of home to a picnic. Choose a fun denim or sailcloth in plaid or print for the cloth, with harmonizing plain napkins; pink the edges.

Father's Day

The third Sunday in June is observed as "Father's Day," a day to honor fathers all over the country. The observance was started in 1910 by Mrs. John Bruce Dodd of Spokane, Washington.

FEATURE FATHER'S HOBBY

For Father's Day, since many fathers enjoy fishing, we suggest having a fresh fish dinner served on a tablecloth made of fish net (see p. 73).

Let your imagination be your guide in planning the table for other hobbies—hunting, golf, coin or stamp collecting, etc. Serve his favorite dinner (broiled steak is many men's choice).

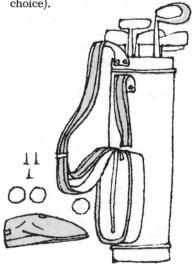

FEAST FOR THE FISHERMAN
Pictured on page 72.

**Fried, Broiled, or Baked Whole Fish
with Tartar Sauce
Buttered Broccoli   Parsleyed Potatoes
Garlic Bread
Relish Tray
Fresh Blueberry Pie**

FRIED, BROILED, OR BAKED WHOLE FISH

**Small whole dressed fish, such as trout, bluefish, butterfish, flounder, herring, mackerel, pike, perch, sea bass, fresh or thawed frozen
Fat (butter gives delicious flavor)**

Dip fish in flour, Bisquick, or corn meal.

To Fry: Fry in hot fat in heavy skillet 5 min., until golden brown on one side; turn, season, and fry 5 min., until golden on other side.

To Broil: Preheat broiler to 550°. Brush fish with fat. Place on broiler rack 3" below source of heat. Broil 5 min.; turn, broil 5 min. more; season.

To Bake: Heat oven to 400° (mod. hot). Place fish in greased shallow pan. Bake 1 to 2 min. per oz.

Serve fish immediately—it becomes soggy on standing. Garnish with lemon wedges and stuffed olive slices for fish eyes.

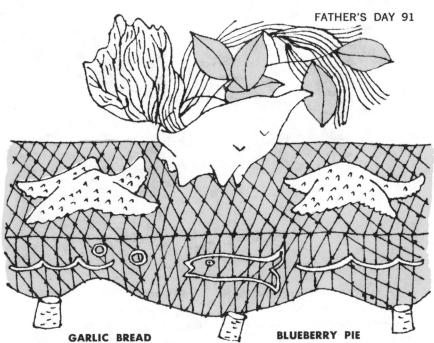

GARLIC BREAD

With sharp knife, cut uniform slices ¾ to 1″ thick from a crusty loaf of French, rye, or Vienna bread. Spread Garlic Butter (below) generously on one side of each slice. Stand upright, close together, in loaf form in bread loaf pan (lined, if desired, with aluminum foil). Fifteen min. before serving time, heat oven to 400° (mod. hot). Heat loaf until piping hot and crusty, about 15 min. Transfer, still in loaf shape, to oblong bread tray and serve at once.

Garlic Butter: Cream butter in a bowl rubbed with a cut clove of garlic. If no garlic is available, cream butter with ½ tsp. garlic salt or a few drops of garlic juice.

BLUEBERRY PIE

	For 9″ Pie	For 8″ Pie
sugar	1 cup	⅔ cup
GOLD MEDAL Flour	⅓ cup	¼ cup
cinnamon	½ tsp.	½ tsp.
fresh blueberries	4 cups	3 cups
lemon juice	1 tbsp.	2 tsp.
butter	1½ tbsp.	1 tbsp.

Heat oven to 425° (hot). Make pastry for 8″ or 9″ two-crust pie using Betty Crocker Instant Mixing Pie Crust Mix or your favorite recipe. Line pie pan. Mix sugar, flour, and cinnamon. Mix lightly through blueberries. Pour into pastry-lined pie pan. Sprinkle with lemon juice. Dot with butter. Cover with top crust which has slits cut in it. Bake *35 to 45 min.*, until crust is nicely browned and juice begins to bubble through slits in crust. Serve slightly warm, not hot.

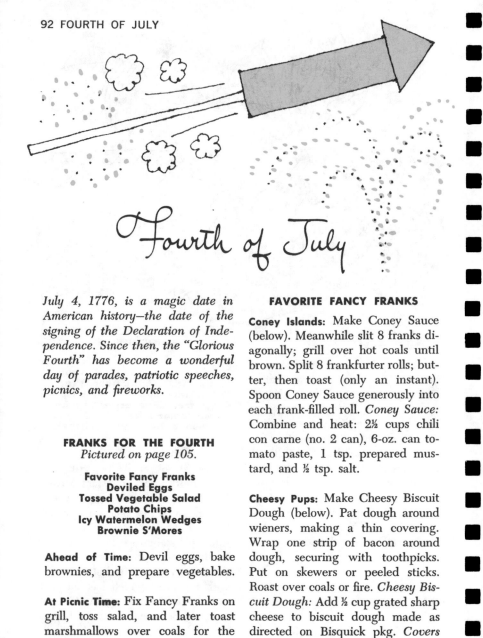

Fourth of July

July 4, 1776, is a magic date in American history—the date of the signing of the Declaration of Independence. Since then, the "Glorious Fourth" has become a wonderful day of parades, patriotic speeches, picnics, and fireworks.

FRANKS FOR THE FOURTH
Pictured on page 105.

Favorite Fancy Franks
Deviled Eggs
Tossed Vegetable Salad
Potato Chips
Icy Watermelon Wedges
Brownie S'Mores

Ahead of Time: Devil eggs, bake brownies, and prepare vegetables.

At Picnic Time: Fix Fancy Franks on grill, toss salad, and later toast marshmallows over coals for the S'Mores.

FAVORITE FANCY FRANKS

Coney Islands: Make Coney Sauce (below). Meanwhile slit 8 franks diagonally; grill over hot coals until brown. Split 8 frankfurter rolls; butter, then toast (only an instant). Spoon Coney Sauce generously into each frank-filled roll. *Coney Sauce:* Combine and heat: 2½ cups chili con carne (no. 2 can), 6-oz. can tomato paste, 1 tsp. prepared mustard, and ½ tsp. salt.

Cheesy Pups: Make Cheesy Biscuit Dough (below). Pat dough around wieners, making a thin covering. Wrap one strip of bacon around dough, securing with toothpicks. Put on skewers or peeled sticks. Roast over coals or fire. *Cheesy Biscuit Dough:* Add ½ cup grated sharp cheese to biscuit dough made as directed on Bisquick pkg. *Covers about 12 franks.*

Stuffed Franks: Split frankfurters lengthwise, almost through. Fill with thin slice of dill pickle or well-seasoned bread stuffing. Wrap each spirally with strip of bacon, fastening with toothpick at each end. Starting with split side down, grill over hot coals until bacon is crisp. Serve in frankfurter rolls.

Frank-a-Bobs: Cut each frank into 5 pieces. Alternate on skewer with pineapple chunks; brush with salad oil. Broil over hot coals, turning until browned. Meanwhile, heat corn muffins in foil over coals. Slip kabob off skewer onto plate. Pass mustard or barbecue sauce and hot buttered corn muffins.

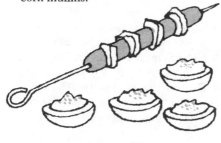

DEVILED EGGS

6 hard-cooked eggs
½ tsp. salt
¼ tsp. pepper
½ tsp. dry mustard
about 3 tbsp. salad dressing or
cream (enough to moisten)

Cut eggs in halves. Slip out yolks. Mash with fork or electric mixer. Add seasonings and salad dressing; continue mashing until smooth. Refill whites with egg yolk mixture, heaping it lightly.

BROWNIE S'MORES

Using Betty Crocker Brownie Mix, spread Fudgy Brownie batter in *two* greased 9" sq. pans or on 15½x12" baking sheet. Bake *15 min.* While warm, cut the contents of each pan into 24 pieces.

At picnic, place two 1" sq. of milk chocolate candy on each of half of the brownies. Toast marshmallows over hot coals or campfire. Slip toasted marshmallow onto chocolate-topped brownie and cover with a plain brownie. *Makes 2 doz.*

BROWNIE TRAY

Arrange brownies, chocolate bar squares, and marshmallows for Brownie S'Mores on a bread board or in a basket. Put small American flags in several brownies here and there.

Or make red and blue marshmallows and arrange with white ones for a patriotic effect. For colored marshmallows: dip in lukewarm water, shake off excess moisture, and roll lightly in colored sugar—some red, some blue.

PICNIC PLATES AND CUPS

If you don't have a set of painted tin picnic dishes, you can make your own. Use scoured tin pie plates (new or used) and tin measuring cups. Paint the name of each family member on the outside of each cup with red ceramic pain, and add a rim of red ceramic pain to each plate.

Children Love to Paint Plates, Too: When children need a rainy day project, set out plates, cups, and paint and let each child paint his own picnic set. What a thrill to eat from his very own picnic plate when the next sunny day rolls around!

RED, WHITE, AND BLUE ACCESSORIES

Your July 4 picnic accessories can be simple and inexpensive when you use blue oilcloth and red bandanas of varying sizes.

Napkins: Small red and white bandanas make practical picnic napkins that can double as bibs for the children. Or fold bandana napkins and tie around picnic silver.

Bandana Bowl-liner: Try lining a large wooden salad bowl with a red and white bandana, knotted in 2 corners; then put in the hot dogs or Favorite Fancy Franks. The effect will be fun and appropriate for outdoor eating.

Tablecloth: Blue oilcloth used on your picnic table finishes your patriotic theme. As glamorous as chintz, yet so practical, oilcloth can be cut with pinking shears; needs no hemming.

Children can spill to their hearts' content, and with the wipe of a cloth you can restore your table cover to its fresh shiny best. If you want to be fancier, sew wide red rickrack along the edge of the cloth.

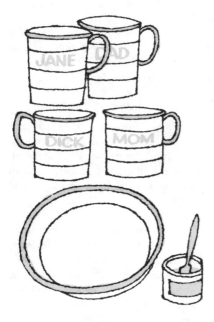

TIPS ON CHARCOAL BROILING

To start: Arrange charcoal in fire box and light. Start about 45 min. before you wish to grill food. When coals are getting hot and almost covered with grey ash, rearrange them, using tongs. At the same time, tap them to remove excess ash and to allow more heat to be given off.

For Steaks, Hamburgers, Most Foods: Arrange coals in checkerboard pattern with empty spaces between for even medium heat.

For Kabobs: Arrange coals in rows. Place kabobs on grill over space between rows of coals to prevent charring.

For a Small Party: Start only a few coals; arrange in one section of fire box.

To Reduce Smoke While Broiling: Trim excess fat from steaks and chops, so fat won't drop and smoke.

Fashion drip pan of heavy duty aluminum foil to place among coals when cooking a large roast or cooking on a spit.

To Douse Flame-ups: Have a baster or clothes sprinkler filled with water; use as needed.

Keep Hands Cool: Chef should wear heavy gloves. Use 1 pair of tongs or pliers to handle hot coals; another to handle food.

ESPECIALLY FOR JULY 4

The day's parade with rippling flags and pounding drums provides symbols (flags, stars, and drums) and colors (red, white, and blue) which can be used in planning and garnishing food for the holiday.

Star Cupcakes: Decorate frosted cupcakes with star designs and, if you wish, dates such as 1776.

Star Cut-outs: Use star cutter not only for cookies but for gelatin salads and sandwiches. With scissors, cut small stars from pimiento and green pepper for meat or salad garnish.

Drum Cake: Use frosted layer cake as drum. Press striped peppermint candy sticks into icing at angles all around cake to simulate drum lacings. Set a maraschino cherry at ends of each stick. Place two sticks of peppermint on top for drum sticks.

INDEPENDENCE DAY SALAD

2 cups cut-up cooked ham (¼" cubes or julienne strips)
4 cups cubed cooked potatoes
2 cups diced celery
1 cup broken-up lettuce
¼ cup finely diced pickle
¼ cup minced green pepper
4 hard-cooked eggs
1 cup mayonnaise
1 tsp. salt
dash of pepper
1 tsp. prepared mustard
¼ cup sour cream or whipped cream

Combine ham, potatoes, celery, lettuce, pickle, green pepper, and 2 of the hard-cooked eggs, sliced. Mix seasonings and cream into the mayonnaise; then carefully blend into ham-and-vegetable mixture. Pile on bed of lettuce and garnish with sprigs of water cress and slices of hard-cooked egg. Add ripe olives and tomato wedges, if desired. *8 to 10 servings.*

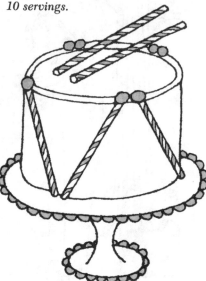

STAR CAKE

Bake Betty Crocker White or Yellow Cake Mix in 8" layer pans as directed on pkg. Cool. Using one layer and toothpicks as a cutting guide, place 5 toothpicks in outside edge to mark the star points (about every 4½"). About 2½" from the edge, place 5 more toothpicks, spacing them evenly between every two toothpicks on the outside edge. Cut out pieces of cake from the outside to the inside toothpicks, forming the star points. Frost star and cut-out pieces with Glaze (recipe below). Arrange star in center of serving plate with pieces around it, the rounded sides toward center. Decorate with small candles stuck in red gumdrops.

Glaze: Heat together ⅓ cup milk and 1 tbsp. white corn syrup. Add this to 1 pkg. Betty Crocker Creamy White Frosting Mix in small mixer bowl and beat until smooth. Add 1 to 2 tbsp. more milk, if necessary.

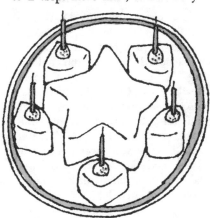

OLD GLORY CAKE

Bake two 9" layers as directed on Betty Crocker Yellow Cake Mix pkg. Cool. Split each layer crosswise into 2 layers. Put cake together using these fillings:

Bottom filling: I cup chilled, canned blueberry pie filling (add ¼ tsp. cinnamon, if desired)

Middle filling: 1 cup sweetened whipped cream*

Top Filling: 1 cup chilled, canned cherry pie filling (add ¼ tsp. almond extract, if desired)

*Whip 2 cups whipping cream with ½ cup *sifted* confectioners' sugar to form firm peaks. Use some for middle filling as directed above. Use remaining cream to frost top and sides of cake.

Decorate top by outlining stars on the top of cake with star cooky cutter. Paint stars blue with extra blueberry pie filling and garnish with silver dragées, if desired. Carefully drizzle cherry filling (liquid part) around edge of top of cake, allowing it to drip down sides. Chill at least 1 hr. before serving.

Note: Use any leftover pie fillings for dessert sauce over pudding or ice cream.

Labor Day

To most of us, Labor Day means a long week end with time for picnics in the backyard, by a lake, or in the autumn woods.

EXCELLENT OUTDOOR EATING

Roman Sandwich
Continental Vegetable Casserole
Tossed Green Salad
Fresh Fruit
Triple Fudge Cake

CONTINENTAL VEGETABLE CASSEROLE
The French call it "Ratatouille"

2 tbsp. olive oil (or salad oil)
1 clove garlic, sliced very thinly
3 small zucchini, sliced ¼" thick
2 med. green peppers, seeded and sliced in rings
1 small eggplant, sliced ¼" thick
2 med. onions, sliced thinly
2 med. tomatoes, sliced thinly

Heat oil in large skillet. Add 1 clove garlic, sliced. Sauté a few moments; then add vegetables in layers in order given, sprinkling each layer with ¼ to ½ tsp. salt and a few grains coarsely ground black pepper. Drizzle another ½ tbsp. oil over top of vegetables. Cover; cook over low heat, gently moving contents from time to time. Cook *35 to 45 min.*, until vegetables are tender and flavors blended. Remove cover last 15 min. to reduce sauce. Serve warm or cold. *6 servings.*

TRIPLE FUDGE CAKE

Heat oven to 350° (mod.). Grease and flour an oblong pan, 13x9½x2". Prepare 1 pkg. chocolate pudding mix (cooked type) as directed on pkg. Blend 1 pkg. Betty Crocker Devils Food Cake Mix (dry mix) into the hot pudding. Batter will be puffy and bubbly. Pour into prepared pan. Sprinkle top of batter with ½ cup semi-sweet chocolate pieces and ½ cup chopped nuts. Bake *30 to 35 min.* Cut in squares; serve warm or cold.

ROMAN SANDWICH

Bake Square Batter Loaf (right). Slice horizontally through center of loaf. Fill generously with moist salami and Provolone cheese. First arrange several layers of cheese, then layers of meat, then more cheese. For variety, try sliced ham or luncheon meat and American, Swiss, or Colby cheese in place of salami and Provolone.

Replace top of loaf and place on large sheet of aluminum foil. Cut 1½" slices crosswise and slice in half down center of loaf, being careful not to cut completely through. Wrap tightly and heat 30 min. in hot oven (425°). Sandwich may be made ahead, wrapped, and refrigerated until ready for use.

To serve: roll down foil, let each person pull out a slice of warm sandwich.

SQUARE BATTER LOAF

1¼ cups warm water (not hot—110 to 115°)
1 pkg. active dry yeast
2 tbsp. soft shortening
2 tsp. salt
2 tbsp. sugar
3 cups *sifted* GOLD MEDAL Flour

In mixing bowl, dissolve yeast in warm water. Add shortening, salt, sugar, and half the flour. Beat 2 min., at med. speed on mixer or 300 vigorous strokes by hand. Scrape sides and bottom of bowl frequently. Add remaining flour; blend with spoon. Cover with cloth and let rise in warm place (85°) about 30 min. (If kitchen is cool, place dough on a rack over a bowl of hot water and cover completely with a towel.)

Beat batter about 25 strokes. Spread evenly in greased 9" sq. glass pan. Pat top in shape with floured hand. Brush with Egg White Glaze (1 unbeaten egg white and 2 tbsp. water) and sprinkle with 1½ tsp. to 1 tbsp. oregano, ½ tsp. salt, and ⅛ tsp. pepper. Let rise again until double, about 40 min. *Heat oven to 350°* (mod.). Bake *45 to 50 min.*, until brown. Remove from pan; cool thoroughly on cooling rack.

Halloween

Halloween today is a mixture of Druid practice, classic mythology, and Christian belief. The Druids believed that ghosts and witches came out on this day, so they built great bonfires to frighten them away. The Roman goddess Pomona, protectress of fruit trees, gave the harvest feature to Halloween. Early Christians adapted the celebration into All Saints' Eve.

Halloween colors are red, orange, and black; red for fire, always feared by witches; orange for the golden harvests; and black for demons and the dreary winter.

TREATS FOR TRICKSTERS

When the neighborhood youngsters, all decked out as ghosts and goblins, come knocking at the door, have a tray of one or more of these easy-to-make goodies ready to pass.

COCOA OR CARAMEL MARSHMALLOW BARS

20 marshmallows
2 tbsp. butter
⅛ tsp. salt
4 cups Cocoa Puffs or
Caramel Puffs

Heat marshmallows, butter, and salt over hot water. Stir until smooth. Pour mixture over Puffs in buttered bowl and mix gently. Pat into greased 9″ sq. pan. Cool; cut into squares.

WITCHCRAFT DOUGHNUTS

4 cups Bisquick
½ cup sugar
⅔ cup milk
2 tsp. vanilla
2 eggs
1 to 2 tbsp. grated orange rind

Heat deep fat to 375°. Mix all ingredients; beat vigorously 25 to 30 strokes. Turn dough onto floured surface and knead about 10 times. Roll out ⅜″ thick. Cut with floured doughnut cutter and place in hot fat. Fry until golden brown, 1 to 2 min. per side. Remove from fat and drain on absorbent paper. Glaze with Thin Chocolate Icing (recipe below). *Makes 24 doughnuts.*

Thin Chocolate Icing: Melt 2 sq. unsweetened chocolate (2 oz.) and 2 tsp. butter over hot water. Remove from heat and blend in 2 cups *sifted* confectioners' sugar and ¼ cup boiling water. Beat only until smooth, not stiff.

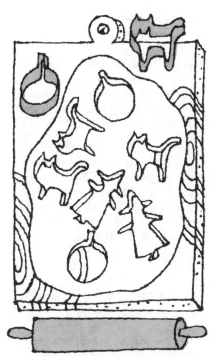

CHILDREN'S HALLOWEEN PARTY

Make Halloween Punch (frozen orange juice with ginger ale). Pass polished red apples and doughnuts or cookies like those on these pages.

BROWNIE-DATE BARS

Heat oven to 350° (mod.). Make Fudgy Brownies as directed on Betty Crocker Brownie Mix pkg.—*except* spread evenly in greased oblong pan, 13x9½x2". Mix well both date and crumb mixture from 1 pkg. Betty Crocker Date Bar Mix, ½ cup hot water, and 1 egg. Spread evenly over brownie batter. Bake *40 to 45 min.* Cool; cut into bars. *Makes 30.*

CANDY-TRIMMED HALLOWEEN COOKIES

Follow directions for Mary's Sugar Cookies (p. 126), making rolled cookies cut with cat, pumpkin, and witch cooky cutters. Frost baked cookies with tinted Easy-creamy Icing (p. 83). Before frosting sets, decorate cookies with candies from an assortment sold at the variety store. For example, attach candy cat's head over cooky cat's head; miniature pumpkins on cooky pumpkins. It's fun to decorate with candies, adding your own whimsical touches.

Children can help cut and decorate the cookies and thus doubly appreciate Halloween treats.

LOLLIPOP COOKIES

Follow directions for Mary's Sugar Cookies (p. 126)—*except* divide dough after mixing and blend 2 sq. semi-sweet chocolate (2 oz.), melted, into one half the dough. Chill. Roll out and cut 2½ to 3" circles. Bake.

Spread Easy-creamy Icing (p. 83) on baked cooky. Place a colored plastic straw or flat wooden stick (tongue depressor) across middle of cooky, with one end extending several inches beyond edge for handle. Place second cooky on top, pressing down slightly. Combine cookies so there will be chocolate, vanilla, and combination lollipops. Decorate with face of tinted and chocolate icing.

Children look forward all fall to their annual rendezvous with ghosts and goblins, black cats, and jack-o'-lanterns. With inexpensive paper decorations and traditional Halloween games and foods, party planning is easy.

WHAT TO DO?

Bob for Apples.

Apple Eating Race: Suspend two small apples from cords in a doorway. Two children race to eat the apple, which swings quickly away as they reach for it. No hands allowed. Tie up 2 more apples for next 2 children.

Treasure Hunt: If weather is fair, have children search for a list of strange ingredients for a witch's magic brew such as stones, leaves, and twigs. The team finding the most items gets the golden treasure —a pumpkin filled with candy or cookies.

If the hunt must be indoors, hide Halloween motifs such as witches' hats cut from black paper about the room. *Or* arrange winding zigzag trails of crepe paper streamers for the guests to follow to the treasure.

Mystery Tales: Gather children in a semi-circle (a crackling fire in the fireplace fascinates them) for an imaginative but not nightmarish mystery story told by dad or an older child.

Older children may want to make a game of telling a Chain Mystery. One child starts an adventure tale, but stops in the midst of the first predicament. He turns to the second child for a solution and the next twist of the tale. And so on around the circle.

Fortune Telling: Here again an obliging grown-up is helpful.

Using tea leaves, palms, or a crystal ball, tell simple fortunes, such as "You will cross water," "You will soon get an important message," etc.

JACK-O'-LANTERN CENTERPIECE

Two-faced Jack: Carve two faces— one happy, one scary—on front and back of a large pumpkin. This is perfect for a round table.

Farmer Jack: Using a large tall pumpkin (odd shapes often sell for less), carve eyes, nose, and mouth. Add small yellow apples for ears, and insert a carrot in nose hole for long pointed nose. Finish with a corn cob pipe and a small basket as a straw hat.

ICE CREAM JACK-O'-LANTERNS

At least 24 hr. before serving, make firm, well-rounded, large scoops of vanilla ice cream. On one side of scoop, use chocolate bits and slices of cherry to make a jack-o'-lantern face. Freeze uncovered until 10 to 15 min. before serving. Just before serving, insert a tiny yellow birthday candle in top of jack-o'-lantern. Serve lighted.

HALLOWEEN SUPPER

Witches' Cauldron Soup
Goblin Franks
Vegetable Relishes
Ice Cream Jack-O'-Lanterns
Milk   Halloween Cookies (p. 101)

Evening Snacks
Hot Buttered Kix and/or Popcorn
Tart Red Apples

WITCHES' CAULDRON SOUP

Serve a simple soup from a large bowl set inside a kettle with a handle which has been covered with black paper. If served in mugs, children can drink broth and spoon out vegetables.

GOBLIN FRANKS

1½ cups *sifted* GOLD MEDAL Flour
1 tsp. baking powder
1 tsp. salt
½ tsp. dry mustard
¼ tsp. paprika
⅛ tsp. cayenne
½ cup corn meal
½ cup shortening
½ to ⅔ cup milk
8 wieners

Heat oven to 450° (hot). Sift flour, baking powder, and seasonings into bowl. Stir in corn meal. Cut in shortening. Stir milk in lightly to make a soft dough. Divide dough into two parts. Roll each into a rectangle about 12x6". Divide dough into 8 parts (4 parts to each half). Place wieners lengthwise on dough, moisten edges of dough, roll up, and seal edges with a fork. Place on baking sheet; sprinkle with paprika. Bake *15 to 20 min.,* or until lightly browned. Serve as a finger food with a dip of catsup or chili sauce.

POPCORN BALLS

Mix in saucepan 1 cup sugar, ⅓ cup water, ⅓ cup light corn syrup, 1 tsp. salt, and ¼ cup butter. Cook to 250° or until a few drops form a hard ball when dropped into cold water. Remove from heat. Stir in 1 tsp. vanilla. Pour in thin stream over 7 cups popped corn in large bowl, stirring constantly to mix well. Shape, with buttered hands, into balls or any other shapes. *Makes 12 to 15 large balls.*

HARD SAUCE SPOOKS

Make Hard Sauce (below). Chill. Shape chilled hard sauce into balls about size of walnuts. Use gumdrops, hard candies, raisins, and candied fruits to make eyes, noses, mouths, and hats on the "spooks." Serve on hot squares of Betty Crocker Gingerbread.

HALLOWEEN REFRESHMENTS

**Hard Sauce Spooks on Gingerbread
Popcorn Balls
Hot Cider with
Cinnamon Stick Stirrers**

HARD SAUCE

Cream ½ cup butter until soft. Blend in gradually 1½ cups *sifted* confectioners' sugar and 2 tsp. vanilla.

FOURTH OF JULY PICNIC

Why not celebrate the Fourth with a gala picnic for your family and friends? On pages 92 through 95 you will find the menu, recipes, and decorating hints for the photograph on the opposite page. And on pages 96 and 97 you will find Fourth of July food specialties.

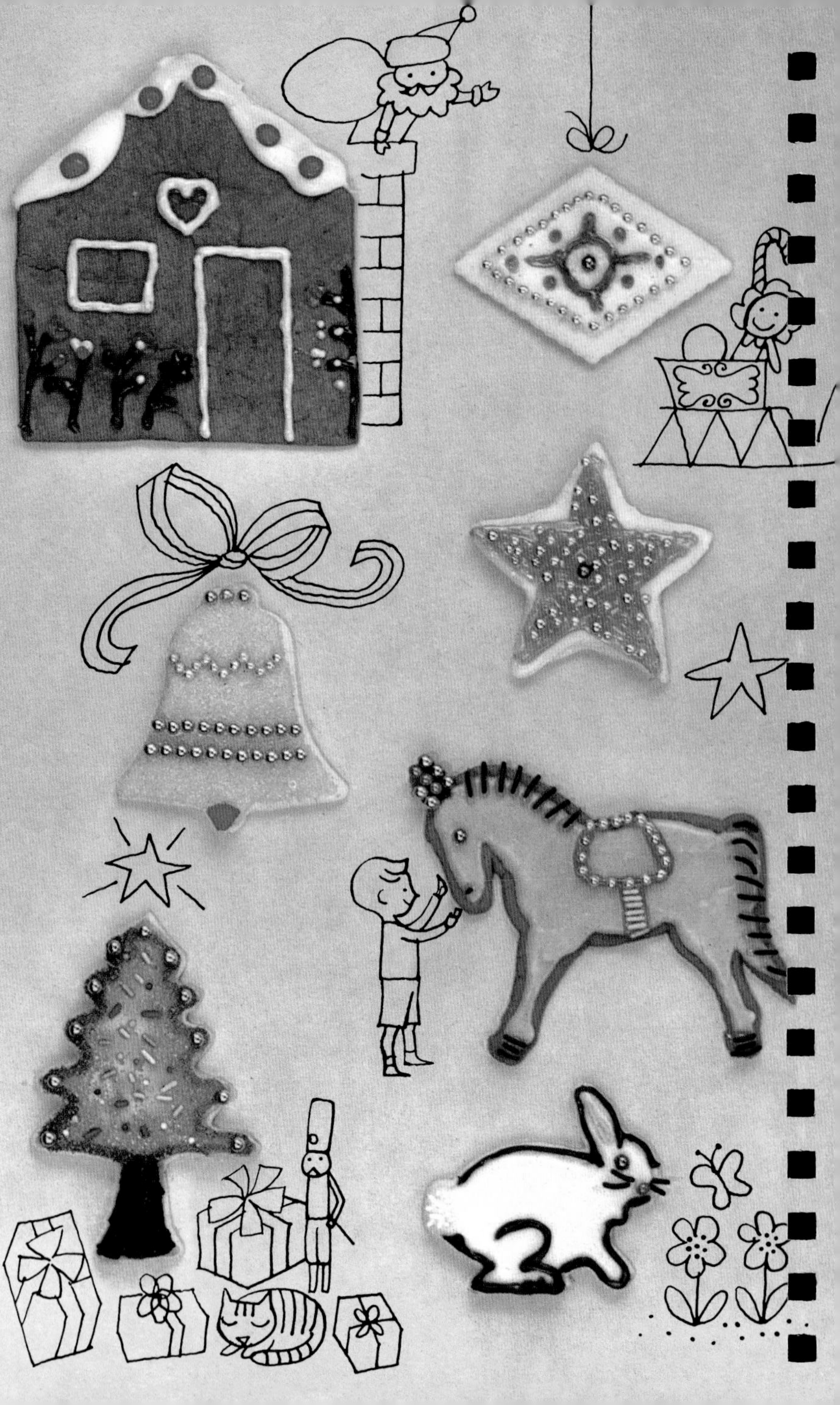

THANKSGIVING GILDED FRUIT CENTERPIECE

You'll need:
  can of gold spray
  fresh pineapple
  variety of fresh fruits and nuts
  greens

Protect area where you will be spraying with lots of newspapers. Wrap pineapple leaves with foil; then spray all of the fruit gold. Allow to dry.

Spread greens in center of table. Fix pedestal for pineapple which will be focal point of arrangement (use a block of wood, footed candy dish, or compote). Pile other gilded fruits around pineapple at random. See that it looks well from all sides.

Since spray keeps air from fruit, it will keep a week or more and could grace a side table after Thanksgiving.

Gilded fruit could also be arranged on a mirror.

You may want to gild artificial fruit and keep it from year to year.

Thanksgiving

This most American of holidays dates back to 1621, when Governor Bradford of Massachusetts instituted December 13 as a day of feasting and prayer for the colonists to give thanks that they were still alive. Women spent days preparing the feast which included wild turkeys, venison, and many corn dishes.

The mother of our modern Thanksgiving is Mrs. Sarah Josepha Hale, editor of the famous Godey's Lady's Book, who worked 17 years for a "national day of thanks."

The very mention of Thanksgiving brings thoughts of warm country kitchens and good things to eat.

ORANGE-FROSTED JACK HORNER CAKE

1 cup cut-up, pitted, uncooked prunes
2 cups *sifted* GOLD MEDAL Flour
1½ cups sugar
1 tsp. salt
1¼ tsp. soda
1 tsp. each cinnamon, nutmeg, and cloves
½ cup cooking (salad) oil
3 eggs (½ to ⅔ cup)
1 cup chopped nuts
2 tbsp. grated orange rind

Pour 1 cup boiling water over cut-up prunes. Let stand 2 hr. *Heat oven to 350°* (mod.). Grease and flour an oblong pan, 13x9½x2"; or two round layer pans, 9x1½". Sift dry ingredients together. Add prune mixture and all other ingredients. Blend thoroughly (about 1 min.). Beat 2 min., med. speed on mixer or 300 strokes by hand. Pour into prepared pan. Bake *oblong 45 to 50 min.; layers 35 to 40 min.* Frost with an orange butter icing.

HARVEST GOLD SALAD

1½ cups carrot juice (12-oz. can)
1 pkg. lemon-flavored gelatin
⅔ cup shredded cabbage
⅓ cup chopped green pepper
⅓ cup chopped onion
1 tbsp. horse-radish
¼ tsp. salt
1 cup crushed pineapple, not drained (8 oz.)

Heat carrot juice and dissolve gelatin in it. Chill until thick and syrupy. (To chill quickly, place pan in bowl of ice water.) Fold in rest of ingredients. Pour into 1-qt. ring mold or individual molds. Chill until firm. Unmold on lettuce and top with mayonnaise. *6 to 8 servings.*

THANKSGIVING DINNER
Pictured on page 108.

Tomato Bouillon
Vegetable Sticks with Cheese Dip
Roast Turkey with
Stuffing of the Region (p. 112)
Chive Mashed Potatoes   Gravy
Jellied Cranberry Sauce
Lima Beans with Mushrooms (p. 113)
Creamed Onions Harvest Gold Salad
Hot Yeast Rolls   Corn Sticks
Jack Horner Cake
Frozen Pumpkin Pie (p. 113)

Ahead of Time: Prepare vegetable sticks and cut up bread and celery for stuffing; bake rolls and cake; prepare pie.

BREAD STUFFING

1 qt. for 4-lb. chicken

4 cups bread cubes or crumbs
⅓ cup butter
¼ cup finely minced onion
½ cup chopped celery
1 tsp. salt
dash of pepper
1 tsp. dried sage, thyme, OR
**   marjoram**
poultry seasoning (to taste)

3 qt. for 12-lb. turkey

12 cups bread cubes or crumbs
1 cup butter
¾ cup finely minced onion
1½ cups chopped celery
1 tbsp. salt
1 tsp. pepper
1 tbsp. dried sage, thyme, OR
**   marjoram**
poultry seasoning (to taste)

Plan a cup of stuffing for each pound of ready-to-cook weight. Prepare cubes or coarse or fine crumbs as desired. Melt butter in heavy skillet. Add onion and cook until yellow (stirring occasionally). Stir in some of bread cubes. Heat, stirring to prevent excessive browning. Turn into deep bowl. Mix remaining ingredients in lightly. For dry stuffing, add little or no liquid. For moist stuffing, mix in just enough hot water or broth to moisten dry crumbs. Cool and place stuffing in bird. Pack stuffing loosely—it swells.

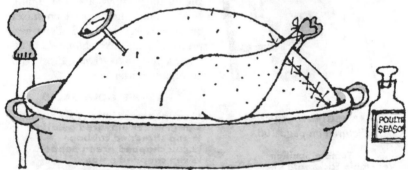

FOUR REGIONAL STUFFINGS

New England Oyster Stuffing: Follow recipe on opposite page—*except* add 1 cup chopped drained oysters for each qt.

Southern Pecan Crumble Stuffing: Follow recipe on opposite page—*except* add ⅔ cup coarsely chopped pecans for each qt.

Midwest Sausage Stuffing: Follow recipe on the opposite page—*except* omit salt and use sausage fat as part of fat. Add ½ lb. bulk pork sausage, crumbled and browned, for each qt.

Far West Apple-Raisin Stuffing: Follow recipe on opposite page—*except* add 1 cup finely chopped apples and ¼ cup raisins for each qt.

FROZEN PUMPKIN PIE

9" baked pie shell
1 cup cooked or canned pumpkin
1¼ cups sugar
½ tsp. salt
½ tsp. ginger
¼ tsp. nutmeg
1 cup whipping cream, whipped
1 pt. vanilla ice cream

Mix pumpkin, sugar, salt, spices.
Fold into whipped cream. Spoon
ice cream into baked pie shell.
Top with pumpkin-cream mixture.
Freeze at least 2 hr. Serve.

LIMA BEANS WITH MUSHROOMS

Cook 2 pkg. frozen green Lima
beans according to directions. Just
before serving, toss with 1 to 1½
cups sliced fresh mushrooms (½ lb.),
sautéed in butter. *6 servings*.

THANKSGIVING DINNER FOR TWO

Shrimp-centered Grapefruit Halves
Cornish Hens with Wild Rice
Cranberry Sauce
Sweet Potatoes   Broccoli Amandine
Tossed Green Salad
Dinner Rolls
Marblehead Cream Pie

MARBLEHEAD CREAM PIE

Follow directions on Betty Crocker Boston Cream Pie Mix pkg.—*except* pour only ⅔ of batter into pan. Stir into remaining batter a mixture of 2 tbsp. cocoa and 2 tbsp. sugar. Spoon here and there over light batter. Cut through batter several times with knife for marbled effect. Bake; fill and frost as directed.

For More Menus and Recipes for Two, see Betty Crocker's Dinner for Two Cook Book.

CORNISH HENS WITH WILD RICE AND ORANGE RAISIN SAUCE

2 frozen Rock Cornish game hens,
    1 to 1¼ lb. each
½ cup wild rice
1½ cups chicken broth
½ tsp. salt
⅓ cup seedless raisins
⅓ cup orange juice
2 tbsp. butter
2 tbsp. flour
½ tsp. salt
dash of pepper
⅛ tsp. paprika
1 cup cream

Thaw hens overnight in refrigerator.

Heat oven to 425° (hot). Rub cavities with salt. Brush hens with melted butter. Bake hens breast-side-up *45 min. to 1 hr.*, or until done. Brush often with butter during baking.

Wash rice and drain well. Simmer rice, chicken broth, and salt in covered saucepan until liquid is absorbed, *30 to 45 min.* Mix raisins and orange juice in small pan. Bring to boil. Reduce heat and simmer 5 min. Melt butter in small skillet. Add flour and seasonings. Cook over low heat, stirring until mixture is smooth and bubbly. Remove from heat. Stir in cream. Bring to boil, stirring constantly. Boil 1 min. Add raisin-orange mixture to sauce. Place hens on beds of wild rice. Pour a little sauce over each hen. Pass extra sauce. *2 servings.*

Chicken Breasts with Wild Rice: Follow recipe above *except* use 4 chicken breasts and double all other ingredients. *4 servings.*

DECORATE WITH FRUITS OF HARVEST

Fall, especially at Thanksgiving, is the perfect time to combine fruits with flowers for unusual decorative effects.

SIMPLICITY IS THE KEYNOTE

First, choose an interesting small container—a china pitcher, a low cut-glass bowl, even an antique iron mortar (part of the set grandmother used to grind spices).

Then, arrange shiny fresh fruits and/or vegetables, gourds, or ears of corn in it. Add flowers or leaves, real or artificial. Let imagination be your guide.

For example, you might combine dark green acorn squash, amber winter onions, dried red peppers, and white or yellow daisies in a low wooden bowl.

Or arrange sprays of wheat with artificial blue or red flowers in an antique iron mortar.

THANKSGIVING ELEGANCE

Gilded fruit makes an elegant yet easy centerpiece, see pages 108-109.

MATCH TABLE AND TURKEY

Table Centerpiece: Use a white compote (or cake stand topped with a shallow bowl). Use a piece of plastic water-holding material, such as Oasis covered with chicken wire, and place it in the compote.

Arrange Fuji mums, pompon mums, and daisies in shades of yellow and white in the compote. Place bunches of green grapes at intervals near the base of the flowers, allowing the grapes to hang over the edge of the compote. Complete with lemon leaves placed at random.

Turkey Garnish: Arrange a circle of shiny green lemon leaves around turkey on platter. Tuck in a few tiny mums and daisies and several small bunches of green grapes here and there. Remove flowers before carving.

Christmas

American Christmas traditions have come from many peoples. English, Italians, French, Germans, Scandinavians, and many others brought their Christmas customs with them.

There are many legends about the origin of the Christmas tree, but we know that the fir tree, lit with candles and hung with gifts, was brought to us from Germany. Our Santa Claus came to us from Holland, where he is known as St. Nicholas, the patron saint of children.

The name of Christmas Day itself goes back to early England when the celebration of Christ's birthday was called "Christe messe," meaning "Christ's mass." And it was the English who originated the custom of saying "Merry Christmas" to friends and neighbors, shouting it from their windows on Christmas morning.

Nowadays we call out our Merry Christmas greetings during the entire Christmas week — and what a friendly way it is to share with others this season of rejoicing!

The following pages include directions and suggestions for house decorations: for front doors, for mantles, for wreaths, and for the children's special "second" Christmas tree. You'll find bright ideas, too, for gift wrapping and tree trimming.

DOOR DECORATIONS

Front Door Greeting: There's no better place to start Christmas decorating than at your front door. Here's a suggestion for adding drama to the usual front door Christmas wreath.

You'll need:
    oilcloth
    a wreath with bow
    cut-out letters

Cover the entire door with red oilcloth. Fold in edges and tack or tape in place. Hang your evergreen wreath with its red satin bow. Then add your personal greeting spelled out in white cut-out letters pasted to the oilcloth. Letters from ½" to several inches in height can be bought at an art or hobby store for a few cents each.

Red and green are traditional colors, but you may want to key your door decorations to the color of your home. For example, try a gold or silver wreath on a door covered with aqua oilcloth.

Cone 'n Leaf Holiday Wreath: Plan an Indian summer outing to gather autumn leaves and pine cones of different shapes and sizes. Later make this handsome wreath for indoors or out.

You'll need:

    corrugated cardboard
    autumn leaves
    pine cones, several types
    walnuts and hazelnuts
    a few red ball ornaments
    gold paint
    linoleum paste

Cut two large doughnut shapes of corrugated cardboard and staple together for base of wreath. For a door, cut the wreath 16" in diameter and 3" wide. Using gold paint and a brush, gild the leaves, a few of the cones, and the nuts.

Paste gilded leaves on entire surface of wreath, using linoleum paste. Then paste on cones, placing some upside down and some sideways for variety. (You may want to dip cones in wood preservative before pasting.) Paste on a few nuts, too. Add a touch of red here and there with red ball ornaments (dip the hook end in the paste). Allow the wreath to dry overnight before hanging.

HOUSE DECORATIONS

Nativity Scene:

You'll need:
  plaster of Paris
  rubber figurine molds
  paint

Children can make the plaster and fill the molds with little guidance from you. When the figures are dry, let the children paint them. Purples, golds, and reds are typical for the garb of Wise Men and the Holy Family.

Candles for the Mantel: Candles are the perfect decoration for your mantel all year 'round, but at Christmas make them special: 6 tiny orange candle cups in a row on a bed of greens; moss green tapers entwined with holly; slim tapers in graduated heights as background for a crèche.

Or try an arrangement of thick round candles in a variety of heights. Choose one color or several according to the color scheme of your room. Tuck greens or cones around the bases. *See picture on page 141.*

Candy and Cooky Wreath: See page 140 for directions.

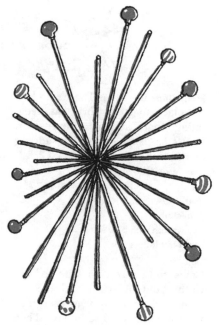

Starburst Mobile:

You'll need:

  colored cellophane drinking straws
  small Christmas balls
  pipe cleaners

Pinch the end of one straw and insert it into the end of a second straw to double the length. Make about 40 of these double straws and tie tightly in the middle with a strong string. Spread the straws so they are evenly spaced. Attach the balls to pipe cleaners and insert into the ends of some of the straws. Suspend from ceiling on a thread. You can also set this on the table as a centerpiece. *See picture on page 141.*

CHRISTMAS TREES
FOR THE CHILDREN

Apple Tree: *Base for apples:* Cut a circle of strong cardboard 10″ in diameter. Glue a 5″ piece of broom handle (or small pole or large dowel) to center of circle. This is the candle support.

Cut a circle 13″ in diameter from pliable cardboard. Cut away ⅓ of it. Form into a cone, overlapping about ½″ (sew or staple together), leaving a center hole large enough to fit over the candle support. Slip cone over candle support and tape or sew to base so it is secure.

Apple arrangement: Wrap 24 medium apples in 10″ sq. of red cellophane, tieing with strong string and leaving ends about 5″ long. Arrange one row of apples on edge of base and tie together tightly so apples lie with bottoms outward. Add a second and third row of apples (each row takes less apples). Wax a 12″ red candle to the top of the support. Fill in all open spaces with small sprays of greens. White pine is one of the prettiest greens for this purpose.

Sugarplum Tree: *Tree:* Cut a 24x15″ rectangle of lightweight cardboard. Starting with one corner, twist to form a cone 15″ tall and 10″ in diameter. Fasten with cellophane tape or paper clips. Trim bottom evenly all around. Set on large plate, tray, or Lazy Susan. Frost with Fluffy White Frosting; trim with candy or frosting decorations. *Pictured on page 141.*

Frosting: Prepare 1 pkg. Betty Crocker Fluffy White Frosting Mix. When frosting stands in high peaks, frost cone. Save 1 cup for decorations.

Candy Decorations: Trim tree with colorful hard candies and silver dragées.

Frosting Decorations: Using the reserved cup of Fluffy White Frosting, blend in 1 to 1½ cups *sifted* confectioners' sugar (add a little at a time until the frosting is stiff enough to hold its shape), 1 tbsp. soft butter, and a dash of salt. Tint Christmas colors. Using pastry tube, make decorations on tree. Use star tip for canes, leaf tip in overlapping fashion for wreaths, and flower tip for stars.

To be able to shape decorations by hand, add sifted confectioners' sugar to frosting until it handles easily.

Cooky Tree: Trim a table-size tree with fancy-shaped cookies.

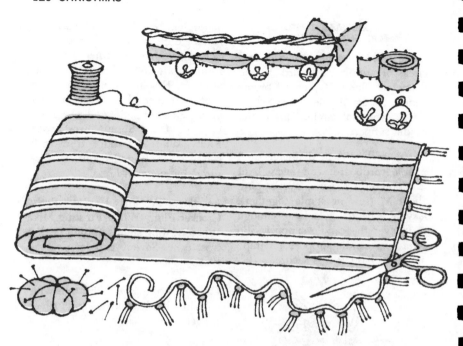

TABLE DECORATIONS

Fun Christmas Runner: Here's how to make a pretty informal Christmas runner to use over a light green or white cloth.

You'll need:
   striped fabric—one width of fabric cut
      the length of your table plus 18"
   ball fringe

Red and white striped fabric with green ball fringe carries out the Christmas colors.

Pin fringe in simple tree shapes on either end of runner; sew on with machine.

Jingle Bells Bread Basket: "Please pass the bread" can bring happy sounds during the holiday season if you tie with ribbon 5 or 6 colored jingle bells onto your bread basket.

Party Apron to Match: Buy extra striped fabric and fringe and make an apron to match your runner. Finish bottom with fringe; pocket is a tree shape.

Victorian Elegance Modern-Style:
You'll enjoy creating a festive holiday tablecloth using one of the new drip-dry fabrics that looks like an elegant old brocade but costs far less.

For plenty of overhang, buy two lengths of fabric, cut one in half lengthwise and sew on either side of remaining length (this avoids center seam in cloth).

Mark cloth edge every 18 to 24". At these marks you'll be drawing up the fabric into a little draped swag (an effect borrowed from draperies). At each mark sew on two 8" long, ¾" wide, bias-cut strips of fabric or matching wide bias tape. Pull matching cords (with tassels, if available) through tapes, leaving ends hanging loosely at bottom edge of cloth.

Then pull up cord, gathering fabric into swag. Secure with pins (pins may be removed so fabric is flat for laundering).

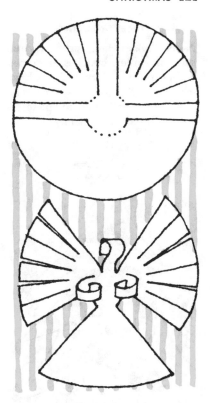

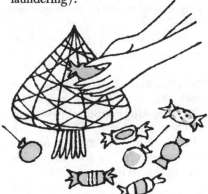

Angel Place Markers: Using clean can lids (from frozen juice or larger food cans), cut with tin snips on lines shown in sketch. Shape into angel, bending back large section for skirt, bending arms forward (to hold candles), and bending back wings and head (see sketch).

Candy Tree Centerpiece: For an easy holiday centerpiece, insert pieces of gaily-colored hard candies into a woven raffia tree. Other novelty Christmas trees can be trimmed with wrapped candies, too.

TREE TRIMMING

Pretty Fruits: Hang artificial fruit such as apples, bunches of grapes, and pears on a white-flocked Christmas tree. Tie red velvet or satin bows to the fruit, and complete the tree with red ball ornaments.

An Old-fashioned Tree: With needle, pierce small holes in ice cream cones and attach string to hang cones on tree. Top cone with cotton batting for realistic, non-melting ice cream. Carry out your old-fashioned tree trim with popcorn balls, candy canes, and strings of cranberries and popcorn.

Cooky Tree: Hang gaily decorated cut-out cookies such as Merry Christmas Cookies on tree with ribbon. You may want to make dark ginger cookies (see directions for Rolled Cookies on Betty Crocker Gingerbread Mix pkg.) to contrast with light sugar cookies.

Beautiful Roses: A long-needled tree such as a Norway pine is best for this trim. Attach artificial roses near the tips of the boughs. Red roses are striking on a white tree, pink ones on a green tree, or pale blue roses on a light blue tree.

MERRY CHRISTMAS COOKIES
Pictured on pages 106-107.

Prepare your favorite sugar cooky dough. Roll ¼″ thick; cut into desired shapes with cooky cutters. Bake as directed. When cooled, frost with Easy-creamy Icing (p. 83). Decorate with sugars, or candied or colored icings.

Christmas Trees: Sprinkle with green sugar; decorate with silver dragées and tiny colored candies.

Santa Claus: Outline shape with red icing; fill bag with tiny colored candies; paint boots with melted chocolate.

Animals: Pipe icing on animals to give highlights to ears, tails, bills, noses; and to give effect of bridles, blankets, etc.

House: Use white icing to mark door, window, and roof; add flowers and other details with colored icing.

Angel: Frost skirt and face white; wings light blue. Trim with gold and silver dragées.

To Hang: Press loop of string into top of cooky before baking. Bake string side *down* on pan.

To Make Paper Decorator Tube: Fill one corner of an envelope with icing; cut off a tiny corner; squeeze.

SANTA CLAUS CUPCAKES
Pictured on page 141.

Bake cupcakes using Betty Crocker White or Yellow Cake Mix. Prepare Betty Crocker Fluffy White Frosting Mix. Color half of the frosting bright red with food coloring.

To frost, place cupcakes upside-down around the edge of a cooling rack. Using white frosting, form a beard, then bring the nose area up into a peak. Put a "red hot" cinnamon candy on the peak for a nose. Make eyes with currants, dipping one side in frosting to make it stick. Place a little white frosting along the top of the cupcake for hair. For a hat, cover the top of the cupcake with red frosting brought up to a point. Add a small piece of marshmallow for a tassel. Leave on the rack until frosting sets.

CHRISTMAS GIFT WRAPPINGS

Little Angel Package Trim: Cover gift box with gold and white patterned paper. Cut out head and wings of an angel from last year's Christmas card collection. Make angel skirt by rolling up a lace paper doily. Glue angel to package and add a pretty bow.

Little Church Package: Fold paper in half to make roof of church; secure to box by tying with yarn. (Pierce holes in roof and box. Pull yarn through; tie with bow on roof side.) Add front and steeple cut from colored paper. Finish with pretty stained-glass window cut from one of last year's Christmas cards.

Ice Cream Cone Trimmed Package: Glue an ice cream cone to any covered package. Fill cone with cotton batting for ice cream. Tie package with fluffy white yarn.

Fruitcake Gift Wraps: Cleaned, empty food cans make fine baking cans for gift fruitcakes. After baking you can simply remove fruitcake, wrap in Pliofilm, and replace in can.

Cover can with a strip of gift wrap paper or wallpaper. You might like pineapple patterned paper trimmed with tiny pieces of plastic fruit from the variety store. Finish the top by gluing narrow green satin ribbon around the edge.

Twice-favored Gift Boxes: *Use sturdy cigar boxes, gaily trimmed: gift boxes today—trinket boxes tomorrow.*

Air the boxes well and you'll never know what they held. Cover and line box with pretty wallpaper.

Glue an inexpensive lace-edged ribbon to edges. Decorate the top of the lid with a Christmas tree ornament, some jingle bells, or holly or evergreen that can be removed when box is used for trinkets.

COOKY SWAP PARTY

This is the easiest way we know of to have a variety of delicious cookies for Christmas entertaining.

Simplify Christmas baking by planning a cooky swap with several friends. Each homemaker bakes a triple batch of her Christmas cooky specialty. Then gather at one home and swap cookies by the dozen.

TOFFEE SQUARES

1 cup butter
1 cup brown sugar (packed)
1 egg yolk
1 tsp. vanilla
2 cups *sifted* GOLD MEDAL Flour
¼ tsp. salt
2 to 3 milk chocolate bars
   (5-cent bars—⅞ oz.)
½ cup chopped nuts

Heat oven to 350° (mod.). Cream together butter, sugar, egg yolk, and vanilla. Stir in flour and salt until dough is thoroughly blended. Spread in rectangle about 13x10" on greased baking sheet. (Leave about 1" all around edge of baking sheet.) Bake *20 to 25 min.*, until nicely browned but still soft. Remove from oven. Immediately place separated sq. of chocolate on top. Let stand until soft. Then spread softened chocolate evenly over entire surface. Sprinkle with nuts. Cut into small squares while warm. *Makes 6 to 7 doz.*

MARY'S SUGAR COOKIES

1½ cups *sifted* confectioners'
   sugar
1 cup butter
1 egg
1 tsp. vanilla
½ tsp. almond flavoring
2½ cups *sifted* GOLD MEDAL Flour
1 tsp. soda
1 tsp. cream of tartar

Mix sugar and butter. Add egg and flavorings; mix until thoroughly blended. Sift dry ingredients together and stir into butter mixture. Refrigerate dough 2 to 3 hr. *Heat oven to 375° (quick mod.).*

For Rolled Cookies: Roll dough on lightly floured pastry cloth to ¼" thick. Cut with cooky cutters. Sprinkle with sugar; place on lightly greased baking sheet. Bake *7 to 8 min.*

For Drop Cookies: Roll dough into small balls. Place 2" apart on lightly greased baking sheet. Bake *about 10 min. Makes 5 doz.*

CHERRY-COCONUT BARS

1 cup *sifted* GOLD MEDAL Flour
½ cup butter
3 tbsp. confectioners' sugar
2 eggs, slightly beaten
1 cup sugar
¼ cup GOLD MEDAL Flour
½ tsp. baking powder
¼ tsp. salt
1 tsp. vanilla
¾ cup chopped nuts
½ cup coconut
½ cup quartered maraschino
   cherries

Heat oven to 350° (mod.). With hands, mix 1 cup flour, butter, and confectioners' sugar until smooth. Spread thin with fingers in sq. pan, 8x8x2". Bake *about 25 min.* Stir all remaining ingredients into eggs. Spread over top of baked pastry (no need to cool). Bake *about 25 min.* Cool. Cut in 3x1" oblongs. *Makes 20 cookies.*

MACAROON SNAPPERS

Mix Betty Crocker Macaroon Mix as directed on pkg. For each macaroon, place 3 pecan halves with ends touching in center on baking paper. Drop rounded teaspoonfuls of dough on center of nuts and bake. While warm, frost with chocolate icing. *Makes 2 doz.*

ORANGE CARAMEL BARS

1½ cups brown sugar (packed)
2 eggs
1⅓ cups *sifted* GOLD MEDAL Flour
⅔ cup cut-up fresh orange
   slices, with white membrane
   left on (1 large or 2 small
   oranges)
⅔ cup cut-up pecans

Heat oven to 350° (mod.). Beat sugar and eggs 3 min., high speed on mixer. Stir in flour. Fold in orange pieces and pecans. Spread thinly in greased jelly roll pan, 15½x10½x1". Bake *30 to 35 min.*, until a golden caramel color and firm to touch. While warm, spread very thinly with *Glaze:* Mix grated rind of 1 orange, ⅔ cup *sifted* confectioners' sugar, and 2 tbsp. cream. Cool in pan. When cool, cut in 2x1½" bars. *Makes 50 bars.*

DATE FRUIT DROPS

Heat oven to 375° (quick mod.). Empty contents of Betty Crocker Date Bar Mix pkg. and date filling envelope into mixing bowl. Add ¼ cup *hot* water and 1 egg; mix well. Stir in 1 cup broken pecans or walnuts, 1 cup candied cherries, cut in halves, and ½ tsp. cinnamon. Drop rounded teaspoonfuls about 2" apart on lightly greased baking sheet. Bake *8 to 10 min. Makes 3 doz.*

SANTA'S LITTLE ELVES PARTY

Plan a party for children 7 to 9 years old to fill baskets or stockings for less fortunate children. Afterward serve this simple supper with a holiday dessert.

Macaroni and Cheese
Carrot Curls   Radish Roses
Celery Sticks   Pickles
Fun Biscuits
Lemon Sherbet   Snowballs
Milk

MACARONI AND CHEESE

4 cups hot drained boiled macaroni (8 oz. uncooked)
3 cups medium white sauce
1¼ cups cut-up mild Cheddar cheese
¼ cup buttered bread crumbs

Heat oven to 350° (mod.). Stir cheese into white sauce until melted. Arrange cooked macaroni and cheese sauce in 8 individual baking dishes in alternate layers. Top with buttered crumbs. Bake *20 min.* Garnish with pimiento stars (cut whole pimiento with cooky cutter or shears). *8 servings.*

FUN BISCUITS

Heat oven to 450° (hot). Make Rolled Biscuit Dough as directed on Bisquick pkg. Turn out on lightly floured board and roll into a rectangle 7½x5½x½". With sharp knife, cut strips ½" wide and 5½" long. Shape into letters, bowknots, people, and animals on ungreased baking sheet. Brush with butter. Bake *10 to 12 min.*

SNOWBALLS

Follow cupcake recipe on Betty Crocker White or Yellow Cake Mix pkg. Spread with prepared Betty Crocker Fluffy White Frosting Mix; roll in shredded coconut. Add a Christmas candle.

HOLIDAY CLUB LUNCHEON

**Surprise Ham Loaves
Whole Kernel Corn with
Julienne Green Beans
Molded Shredded Lettuce
and Vegetable Salad
Butterhorn Rolls   Jelly
Icelandic Terta**

For a Lighter Luncheon: Omit either the vegetable or salad.

For a Dinner Meeting: Add Golden Roast Turkey (it isn't necessary to stuff it).

SURPRISE HAM LOAVES

Heat oven to 350° (mod.). Drain pickled peaches or apricots. Make your favorite ham loaf mixture. Fill greased custard or muffin cups half full with ham mixture. Put one pickled peach or apricot in center of each cup. Add more ham mixture to make cup ¾ full. Bake *45 to 60 min.*

ICELANDIC TERTA

Heat oven to 350° (mod.). Make batter as directed on Betty Crocker Yellow Cake Mix pkg.—*except* add 1½ tsp. *freshly ground* cardamom seed to mix before adding liquid. Divide batter into 4 greased and floured round layer pans, 9x1½". Bake two layers at a time, putting other two in refrigerator until time to bake. Bake *15 to 20 min.* Cool. Fill with Date-Fig Filling (below) and sprinkle top of cake with *sifted* confectioners' sugar. *12 servings.*

Date-Fig Filling

**two 6½-oz. pkg. dates, chopped
(2 cups)
½ cup finely chopped figs
1 cup sugar
1½ cups water**

Cook ingredients together until thick. Cool before spreading between layers.

CHRISTMAS EVE SUPPER

Christmas Eve is usually a family night, spent trimming the tree and singing carols. Serve a simple supper so that you will have plenty of time for decorating the tree.

**Oyster Stew or
Creamy Corn Chowder
Egg or Ham Salad Sandwiches
Crisp Greens with Pimiento
French Dressing
Old-fashioned Baked Pears
Warm Sugared Gingerbread**

OLD-FASHIONED BAKED PEARS

**6 d'Anjou or Bosc pears
¾ cup brown sugar (packed)
½ cup maple syrup
⅓ cup water
⅛ tsp. salt
⅛ tsp. ginger
grated rind of 1 lemon**

Heat oven to 325° (slow mod.). Wash pears. Cut thin slice from blossom end so pears will stand easily. Leave stems on. Place pears upright in 9" sq. baking dish. Mix remaining ingredients and pour over pears. Bake uncovered *about 1½ hr.*, or until pears are tender. Baste syrup over pears occasionally while baking. Serve slightly warm or chilled with syrup.

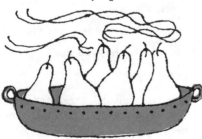

WARM SUGARED GINGERBREAD

Bake easy-to-make Betty Crocker Gingerbread Mix. While warm, sprinkle with granulated sugar.

"ON CHRISTMAS DAY IN THE MORNING"

Make the family breakfast very special by serving it near the excitement of the Christmas tree. After the children have opened their gifts, scramble eggs right at a card table in an electric fry pan and serve them in this novel way.

**Orange Juice
Creamy Scrambled Eggs
with Special Garnishes
Honeycomb Coffee Cake
or a Traditional Christmas Bread**

SCRAMBLED EGGS WITH SPECIAL GARNISHES

Arrange small bowls of julienne ham, shredded cheese, pineapple marmalade, sautéed mushrooms, and chopped green pepper on a tray. Each one sprinkles one or more of the garnishes over his serving of hot creamy scrambled eggs.

If You Wish to Serve Soft-cooked Eggs, use egg cups; add a Christmas touch by putting a holiday sticker on each shell, or a tiny Christmas wreath around each egg.

HONEYCOMB CAKE

**2 cans Betty Crocker Bisquick
  Refrigerated Biscuits
½ cup light brown sugar (packed)
1 tbsp. flour
1 tsp. cinnamon
½ cup butter, melted
¼ cup chopped walnuts
¼ cup chopped dates
¼ cup honey**

Heat oven to 350° (mod.). Combine sugar, flour, cinnamon, ¼ cup melted butter, walnuts, and dates. Place 10 biscuits in an ungreased 2-qt. baking dish. Top with sugar mixture. Place remaining 10 biscuits on sugar mixture. Combine honey and remaining ¼ cup butter. Pour over biscuits. Bake *40 to 45 min.* Leave in baking dish about 10 min.; invert on serving plate.

CHICKEN FOR CHRISTMAS DINNER

**California Cream Soup
Roast Stuffed Capon or Chicken
Gravy   Mashed Potatoes
Warm Spiced Crab Apples
ringed with Broccoli Spears
Gourmet Tossed Green Salad
Parkerhouse Rolls
Sparkling Cranberry Sherbet
Yuletide Chiffon Cake**

Ahead of Time: Cut up bread and celery for stuffing, slice and break up vegetables for salad, and bake cake. Make soup ahead, if you like.

CALIFORNIA CREAM SOUP

**10½-oz. can cream of celery soup
10½-oz. can cream of chicken soup
⅔ cup light cream
2 cups milk
¾ tsp. salt
⅛ tsp. pepper
¾ cup chopped avocado
¼ cup ripe olives, sliced
¼ cup chopped pimiento**

Mix soups, cream, milk, salt, and pepper in large saucepan. Cook over low heat to simmer. Stir in remaining ingredients. Continue heating slowly for several min. *Makes 7½ cups: 4 main dish or 6 to 8 first course servings.*

GOURMET TOSSED GREEN SALAD

**1 med. head lettuce
1 small head cauliflower
1 small, sweet Bermuda onion
1 med. green pepper, diced
1 pimiento, diced (about 3 tbsp.)
6 large fresh hothouse
    mushrooms, washed and thinly
    sliced (about 1 cup)
½ cup pitted green olives, sliced
½ cup Roquefort cheese,
    crumbled
1 clove garlic, crushed and grated
Classic French Dressing
    (recipe below)**

Tear lettuce into bite-size pieces. Wash cauliflower and remove green stalks. Separate into tiny flowerets. Cut onion in paper-thin rings. Toss gently with green pepper, pimiento, mushrooms, olives, and cheese. Chill about *1 hr.* Toss and serve immediately with Classic French Dressing.

Classic French Dressing: Mix 2 tbsp. cooking (salad) oil, 2 tbsp. white wine (tarragon) vinegar, 1 clove garlic, pressed and minced, 1¼ tsp. salt, dash of freshly ground pepper, and dash of flavor extender. *6 to 8 servings.*

SPARKLING CRANBERRY SHERBET

Sprinkle a few silver dragées over each scoop of cranberry sherbet.

YULETIDE CHIFFON CAKE

1 pkg. Betty Crocker Orange
   Chiffon Cake Mix
¾ cup finely cut mixed candied
   fruit
½ cup finely chopped nuts

Prepare cake batter as directed on pkg. Fold fruit and nuts into batter and pour into a 10" tube pan. Bake as directed. Frost top and sides with Mint Cream Topping.

Mint Cream Topping: Whip ¼ cup green or red mint jelly with fork until it forms a thin syrup. Whip 1½ cups whipping cream with ¼ cup *sifted* confectioners' sugar. Fold jelly into whipped cream. Frost top and sides of cake. Whip 2 more tbsp. jelly to swirl through frosting.

LAMB FOR CHRISTMAS DINNER

**Crabmeat Cocktail or
Oysters on the Half Shell
Party Lamb Chops
Twice-baked Potatoes
Parsley-buttered Rutabagas
bordered with Green Peas
Grapefruit-Avocado Salad
Butterhorn Rolls
Nesselrode Pie with Meringue Shell**

Ahead of Time: Bake meringue, fill, and freeze; bake, mash, refill, and refrigerate potatoes; prepare cocktail sauce.

OYSTERS ON THE HALF SHELL

Allow 6 oysters per serving. Have shells opened by the fish dealer. Serve each oyster on half of shell; arrange on bed of crushed ice. Center each plate with small container or bit of lettuce filled with a tangy cocktail sauce.

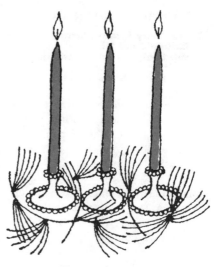

PARTY LAMB CHOPS

**eight 1″ thick loin or shoulder
   lamb chops, boned
8 thin slices large onion
8 thin slices processed Swiss
   cheese
½ cup commercial sour cream**

Heat oven to 325° (slow mod.). Season chops generously on both sides with salt. Place in roasting pan. Place 1 onion slice, 1 cheese slice, and 1 tbsp. sour cream on each chop. Bake uncovered *30 min.;* cover and bake *2 hr. longer,* or until tender. *8 servings.*

NESSELRODE PIE
WITH MERINGUE SHELL

10″ round Meringue Shell (below)
2 qt. softened vanilla ice cream
5-oz. jar commercially prepared
**   Nesselrode mixture**
½ cup flaked coconut
½ cup toasted almonds
⅓ cup chopped candied cherries
**   (red and green, if desired)**

Bake meringue shell, cool. Fill with mixture of remaining ingredients. Freeze overnight. Thaw about ½ hr. before serving. *10 to 12 servings.*

MERINGUE SHELL

3 egg whites
¼ tsp. cream of tartar
1 cup sugar

Beat egg whites and cream of tartar until frothy. Beat in sugar, a little at a time. Beat until very stiff and glossy. Spread on heavy brown paper on baking sheet in one large round or heart or 8 individual shells, shaping and building up edges with back of spoon. *Heat oven to 275° (slow).* Bake *60 min.* Turn off oven and leave in until cool.

BEEF FOR CHRISTMAS DINNER

Cream of Artichoke Soup
Roast Prime Ribs of Beef
Duchess Potatoes   Orange Beets
Asparagus with Caper Butter
Holiday Relishes   Crisp Bread Sticks
English Plum Pudding
with Hard Sauce
or **Assorted Fruit Ices**

Ahead of Time: Prepare soup, beets, and hard sauce and refrigerate; prepare relishes; bake bread sticks.

CREAM OF ARTICHOKE SOUP

A rich special-occasion soup.

1 buffet-size can artichoke hearts, drained
10½-oz. can cream of chicken soup
2 cups milk
1 cup cream
2 cups chicken broth
1 to 2 bay leaves, if desired (in cheesecloth sack)
freshly ground black pepper

Slice artichoke hearts crosswise. Mix all ingredients. Heat just to boil. Remove sack of bay leaves just before serving. *6 servings.* (Note: This soup can be made ahead of time, refrigerated, and reheated just before serving.)

ORANGE BEETS

¼ cup sugar
2 tbsp. vinegar
1 tsp. salt
2 no. 303 cans sliced beets (drain, saving ⅔ cup beet juice)
2 small onions, sliced in thin rings
4 tsp. grated orange rind
⅔ cup fresh orange juice

Mix all ingredients, including ⅔ cup beet juice, in bowl and refrigerate several hr. or overnight. Remove from refrigerator. Cook beets in saucepan over med. heat. Serve immediately. *6 to 8 servings.*

CAPER BUTTER

Melt ½ cup butter, add 2 tsp. white vinegar, 1 tbsp. bottled capers, and a little chopped parsley. Serve warm over asparagus. *Makes ½ cup.*

HOLIDAY RELISHES

Arrange pickled mushrooms, green olives, red radishes, celery sticks, and green pepper stars on a pretty relish tray—perhaps a two-tiered tray. Cut stars from seeded green pepper with kitchen shears or cooky cutter.

SUPPER STARRING LEFTOVERS

Stuffed Turkey Slices
Cranberry Sauce
Fresh Frozen Peas with Orange Butter
Crisp Cole Slaw   French Bread
Camembert Cheese
Fruitcake

ORANGE BUTTER

Flavor melted butter with grated orange rind.

STUFFED TURKEY SLICES

2 cups leftover mashed potatoes
    or 1 packet (½ pkg.) Betty
    Crocker Instant Mashed
    Potatoes
1 egg, slightly beaten
½ cup herb-seasoned bread
    stuffing
¼ cup chopped parsley
½ tsp. salt
dash of pepper
¼ cup butter
1 med. onion, chopped (½ cup)
½ cup diced celery
8 to 10 large slices cooked turkey
½ cup stock or broth

Heat oven to 425° (hot). Heat mashed potatoes or prepare according to pkg. directions; beat in egg. Add bread stuffing, parsley, salt, and pepper. Melt butter in small skillet; sauté onion and celery until tender; add to potato mixture.

For each serving, cut an oval of aluminum foil about 13x7" (size depends on size of turkey slice). On half of foil place slice of turkey, spread with potato mixture, and top with second turkey slice. Pour 2 tbsp. broth over turkey. Close and seal foil by folding the two edges together. Repeat for remaining servings. Place on baking sheet. Bake 20 to 25 min., until heated through. To serve: cut slits in top of foil and fold back. Serve with cranberry sauce. 4 to 5 servings.

SKATING OR CAROLING PARTY

Hot Ham 'n Swiss Cheese Sandwiches
Oriental Burgers
Christmas Relish Tree
Cocoa Chiffon Cake
Fresh Fruit Compote

Ahead of Time: Make, wrap, and refrigerate ham and cheese sandwiches; prepare Oriental Burger mixture; bake cake; combine and refrigerate fruits; prepare relishes.

CHRISTMAS RELISH TREE

Use a three-tiered serving tray or set a small compote atop a footed cake plate. Fill with all sorts of crisp relishes: pickles, stuffed celery, carrot sticks, olives. Top with a star tree ornament.

ORIENTAL BURGERS

1 med. onion, sliced
1 lb. ground beef
2 tbsp. cooking (salad) oil
1 can bean sprouts, drained
5-oz. can water chestnuts, sliced
  (¾ cup)
⅓ cup soy sauce
⅓ cup water
1 tbsp. dark molasses
2 tbsp. cornstarch
2 tbsp. water
hamburger buns

Sauté onion and beef in oil until browned. Add bean sprouts, water chestnuts, soy sauce, ⅛ cup water, and molasses. Cook about 5 min. Add 2 tbsp. water to cornstarch; mix and add to mixture. Bring to boil; boil 1 min. Salt to taste. Serve in hamburger buns. *Makes about 8 sandwiches.*

HAM 'N SWISS CHEESE SANDWICHES

Split and butter hamburger buns. Spread one side with prepared mustard and pickle relish, if desired. Insert a slice of baked or boiled ham and one of processed Swiss cheese. Wrap sandwiches in foil; refrigerate. Before serving, place foil-wrapped buns on baking sheet. Heat *20 to 25 min.* in mod. oven (350°). Serve in foil wrappings from a big basket.

HOLIDAY BUFFET

One day between Christmas and New Year's, plan a festive buffet dinner party for two or three favorite families. The children will never know the whole party wasn't planned especially for them as they enjoy their own dinner at a separate table (p. 147).

Fruit on a Pick
Baked Ham
Crab and Shrimp Casserole
Limas with Green Pepper
Cheese-scalloped Asparagus
Relishes on Ice
Red 'n Green Fruit Molds
Biscuit Christmas Tree
Orange Yuletide Tarts

Ahead of Time: Prepare Orange Fluff Filling and Fruit Molds and chill; bake Tart Shells; make Cheese Sauce and crush crackers for asparagus casserole; chop vegetables for sea food casserole; prepare relishes.

CRAB AND SHRIMP CASSEROLE

1 med. green pepper, chopped
1 med. onion, chopped
1 cup chopped celery
6½-oz. can crabmeat, flaked
4½-oz. can shrimp, cleaned and flaked
½ tsp. salt
⅛ tsp. pepper
1 tsp. Worcestershire sauce
1 cup mayonnaise
1 cup buttered crumbs

Heat oven to 350° (mod.). Mix all ingredients. Place in greased 1-qt. baking dish. Sprinkle with crumbs. Bake *30 min. 8 servings.*

RED 'N GREEN FRUIT MOLDS

Serve Cranberry and Lime Fruit Cream Molds side by side or interlocking on lettuce or other greens. Have a bowl of fruit dressing nearby so guests may help themselves. *18 to 20 servings.*

Cranberry Cream Mold: Dissolve 3 pkg. raspberry-flavored gelatin in 3 cups hot water. When mixture begins to set, beat in 1 pt. commercial sour cream and 2 cups sweetened whole cranberry sauce. Pour into 1½-qt. ring mold; chill until firm.

Lime-Pineapple Cream Mold: Follow recipe above—*except* use lime-flavored gelatin and pineapple tidbits in place of raspberry gelatin and cranberry sauce.

Recipes continued on page 146.

CANDY AND COOKY WREATH

Obtain a variety of candy, cookies, and nuts (75 to 100 pieces). Cut squares of Pliofilm at least 2″ larger than candy, cooky, or nut to be wrapped. Wrap each piece and secure Pliofilm with 1 or 2 twists; tie a 6″ piece of gift wrap ribbon around each piece. Shape wire coat hanger into circle. With hanger lying flat on table, tie on ribbons with candies, etc., selecting a variety of shapes and colors, until hanger is filled. Using a scissors blade flat in your hand, curl all loose ribbon ends. Tuck in sprigs of holly or greens, if you wish. Tie a large bow at bottom of wreath. Wreath can be used as table centerpiece or door decoration. If used on a door, add a small pair of blunt children's scissors so passersby can cut off a candy, cooky, or nut.

Candies: Squares or balls of fudge rolled in chopped nuts. Balls of fondant rolled in colored sugar. Wrapped candies such as red and white peppermints, assorted hard candies, bubble mints.

Cookies: Red or green macaroons. Russian teacakes. Brownies cut in 1″ squares. Star-shaped pressed cookies wrapped back to back.

Sugar Plum Tree (p. 119)

Starburst Mobile (p. 118)

Santa Claus Cupcakes (p. 123)

(see pp. 150-151)

BRIDAL SHOWER BRUNCH

More and more hostesses are entertaining at brunch—that happy combination of breakfast and lunch. Invite guests for 10:30 or 11 A.M.

Bouquet Fruit Cocktail (p. 74)
Cheese Soufflé
with Creamed Chicken
Blueberry Streusel Coffee Cake
Coffee

CHEESE SOUFFLÉ

¼ cup Bisquick
½ tsp. dry mustard
1 cup milk
1 cup grated cheese
3 eggs, separated
¼ tsp. cream of tartar

Heat oven to 350° (mod.). Mix Bisquick and mustard. Add a small amount of milk to Bisquick in saucepan to make paste. Add the rest of the milk gradually. Bring to boil; boil 1 min., stirring constantly. Stir in cheese; remove from heat. Add to slightly beaten egg yolks. Beat egg whites and cream of tartar until stiff enough to hold soft peaks. Fold into cheese mixture. Pour into ungreased 1½-qt. baking dish placed in pan of hot water. Bake *50 to 60 min.*, or until silver knife comes out clean when inserted near center. *4 to 6 servings.*

PATTY PITCHER, THE BRIDE'S MAID

Select a tall slim pitcher as your gift to the bride-to-be.

Fill pitcher with excelsior. Push a cork into the center of a round vegetable brush. Stand the brush handle in the excelsior in pitcher so brush becomes head. Widen neck with piece of florist's clay around brush handle nearest brush; cover clay with ribbon.

Using a double lace paper doily, finger pleat a ruffly collar. Fashion apron with another double doily, and sash of glossy gift tie ribbon. Complete figure with plastic scrub pad hat, button eyes and mouth (secured with white glue), artificial flower earrings, and hat decoration. Arrange with several household sponges.

BLUEBERRY COFFEE CAKE

Heat oven to 400° (mod. hot). Make muffin batter using Betty Crocker Wild Blueberry Muffin Mix; pour batter into greased 8″ sq. pan. Sprinkle with Streusel (below). Bake *20 to 22 min. 9 servings.*

Streusel: Using fingers or fork, mix ⅓ cup brown sugar (packed), ⅓ cup flour, ¼ cup cold butter, and ½ tsp. cinnamon.

ORANGE YULETIDE TARTS

Make Pastry Tart Shells using **Betty Crocker Instant Mixing Pie Crust Mix** or your favorite recipe. Fill with cooled Orange Fluff Filling. Garnish with candied cherries and Chocolate Leaves.

ORANGE FLUFF FILLING

½ cup sugar
2 tbsp. cornstarch
¾ cup orange juice (use frozen concentrated orange juice, diluted according to directions)
2 large egg yolks, slightly beaten
1 tbsp. butter
2 egg whites
¼ tsp. cream of tartar
¼ cup sugar

Mix sugar and cornstarch in saucepan. Gradually stir in orange juice. Cook over mod. heat, stirring constantly, until mixture thickens and boils. Boil 1 min. Remove from heat. Beat at least half of hot mixture into egg yolks. Then beat into remaining hot mixture. Return to heat and boil 1 min., stirring constantly. Remove from heat. Continue stirring until smooth. Blend in butter. Make meringue by beating egg whites and cream of tartar until frothy; gradually beat in sugar. Fold meringue into orange mixture. Cool. *Enough to fill 12 tarts.*

CHOCOLATE LEAVES

Wash and dry 2 doz. leaves of varying sizes. Melt 2 sq. semi-sweet chocolate (2 oz.) or ½ cup semi-sweet chocolate pieces into 1 tsp. butter. Paint chocolate on backs of leaves about ⅛″ thick and just to the edges. Chill until firm. Peel leaves off chocolate; arrange on tarts.

CHEESE-SCALLOPED ASPARAGUS

2 pkg. frozen cut-up asparagus, thawed
½ cup toasted, slivered almonds
½ tsp. salt
dash of pepper
Rich Cheese Sauce (below)
1 cup soda cracker crumbs

Heat oven to 350° (mod.). Put half of asparagus in 2-qt. baking dish. Top with half the amounts of rest of ingredients in order listed. Cover with remaining asparagus and top with rest of ingredients. *Bake 40 to 45 min. 6 to 8 servings.*

Rich Cheese Sauce: Make 2 cups medium white sauce with ¼ cup butter, ¼ cup flour, 1 tsp. salt, and 2 cups milk. Stir in 1 cup cut-up or grated nippy American cheese, 1 tsp. dry mustard, and 1 tsp. Worcestershire sauce.

SPECIAL CHILDREN'S DINNER

**Fruit on a Pick
Sliced Baked Ham
Mashed Potatoes   Stewed Tomatoes
Crisp Relishes
Little Biscuit Tree
Orange Fluff Dessert**

Center children's table with second Christmas tree (p. 119). Have place cards for all, and bibs for the tiniest ones.

ORANGE FLUFF DESSERT

Fill serving dishes with Orange Fluff Filling (p. 146). Fold in or garnish with banana slices, orange sections, and maraschino cherries.

BISCUIT CHRISTMAS TREE

Heat oven to 450° (hot). Separate biscuits from two cans Betty Crocker Refrigerated Biscuits. At center top of ungreased baking sheet, place a biscuit, then make two rows of 2 below, then two rows of 3 and two rows of 4 biscuits, making "tree" shape as you go along. Final biscuit is made into an oval and placed at the center bottom as base. Bake *10 to 12 min.*, or until golden brown. Frost while hot with light green confectioners' sugar glaze. Put large whole maraschino or candied cherries in hollows where biscuits come together and cherry halves on edges and at peak of tree. Sprinkle with green colored sugar.

LITTLE BISCUIT TREE

Follow recipe above—*except* use one can of biscuits. Place a biscuit at top of baking sheet, then 2 below, then two rows of 3 biscuits. Pat slightly into tree shape. Final biscuit is shaped into oval for base. Bake and decorate as for Biscuit Christmas Tree (above).

PROGRESSIVE PARTY FOR TEENS

The high school crowd will enjoy sharing the fun as well as the cost and preparation of one big holiday party. And it's so easy when it's shared.

Plan the menu for 16. Divide it into three courses, each to be served at a different house. Then end the evening at a fourth house, with dancing and caroling. Since the main course is most costly, the responsibility for it could be shared by four couples.

Pizzarinos
Fruit-flavored Soft Drinks

Easy Oven-fried Chicken
Baked Potatoes
Creamed Peas and Onions
Relish Tray
Herb-buttered Bread

Pink Parfaits or Sundaes
Brownie Fudge Layer Cake

PIZZARINOS

1 can Betty Crocker Refrigerated Pizza
½ cup finely diced Mozzarella cheese
⅔ cup sliced pepperoni

Heat oven to 425° (hot). Cut roll of dough into 8 slices. Places slices on lightly greased baking sheet, 15x12″. Pat into 4 or 4½″ rounds. Spoon tomato sauce onto individual rounds and top with slices of pepperoni and Mozzarella cheese. Bake *12 to 15 min. Makes 8 individual pizzas.* Double or triple the recipe for 16 hungry teenagers.

BROWNIE FUDGE LAYER CAKE

1 pkg. Betty Crocker Brownie Mix
½ cup water
2 eggs, unbeaten
½ cup chopped nuts

Heat oven to 350° (325° for glass pans). Grease two 8″ layer pans. Empty brownie mix into small mixing bowl. Blend in ¼ cup water and eggs. Beat 1 min., med. speed on mixer or 150 vigorous strokes by hand. Scrape sides and bottom of bowl often. Blend in another ¼ cup water. Beat 1 more min., scraping bowl. Fold in nuts. Pour into prepared pans. Bake *20 to 25 min.* Cool. Fill and frost with 1 pkg. Betty Crocker Chocolate Fudge Flavor Frosting Mix. Garnish top with walnut halves.

MERRY MORNING COFFEE PARTY

**Little Anadama Loaves
Individual Butter Pats
Green Grapes or other Fresh Fruit
Little Wedges of Sharp Cheese
Christmas Cookies (p. 123)
Hot Mocha Java**

HOT MOCHA JAVA

Prepare both hot coffee and hot chocolate. Fill cups half full of the chocolate; then fill cup with steaming coffee.

LITTLE ANADAMA LOAVES

¾ cup boiling water
½ cup yellow corn meal
3 tbsp. shortening
¼ cup molasses
2 tsp. salt
¼ cup warm water (not hot— 110 to 115°)
1 pkg. active dry yeast
1 egg
2¾ cups *sifted* GOLD MEDAL Flour

Stir together in large mixer bowl, boiling water, corn meal, shortening, molasses, and salt. Cool to lukewarm. Dissolve yeast in warm water. Add yeast, egg, and half the flour to lukewarm mixture. Beat 2 min., med. speed on mixer or 300 vigorous strokes by hand. Scrape sides and bottom of bowl frequently. Add rest of flour and mix with spoon until flour is thoroughly blended into dough. Spread batter evenly in 6 miniature greased loaf pans, 4¾x2⅝x1½″. Batter will be sticky. Smooth out tops of loaves by flouring hand and patting into shape.

Let rise in warm place (85°) until batter just reaches tops of pans— about 1½ hr. Sprinkle top with a little corn meal and salt.

Heat oven to 375° (quick mod.). Bake *30 to 35 min.* To test loaf, tap the top crust; it should sound hollow. Crust will be dark brown. Immediately remove bread from pans. Place on cooling rack or across edges of bread pans. Brush tops with melted butter. Cool before cutting.

EGGNOG AND WASSAIL PARTY
Pictured on page 142-143.

At one end of the table serve wassail and the tart tidbits that are so good with it. At the other end, have a bowl of eggnog encircled by sweet dainties.

Hot Wassail Bowl
Shrimp-Anchovy Sandwiches
Tangy Holiday Dip
with Potato Chips
Celery Stuffed with Cheese and
Bacon Bits

Chilled Eggnog
Slices of Mystery Fruitcake
Caramel Meringue Bars
and other Holiday Cookies
Warm Toasted Cashews

SHRIMP-ANCHOVY SANDWICHES

Cut about 6 slices bread into 15 or 16 rounds, using a 1¾" cutter. Toast if desired. Spread with Anchovy Butter (a mixture of 2 tsp. anchovy paste with 3 tbsp. butter) and top with whole, canned shrimp (4½-oz. can). *Makes 15 or 16.*

TANGY HOLIDAY DIP

two 8-oz. pkg. cream cheese,
** softened**
1 tbsp. garlic wine vinegar
1 tbsp. onion juice
1 tbsp. Worcestershire sauce
about ½ tsp. Tabasco sauce
¼ cup catsup
¼ cup salad mustard

Blend all ingredients. Serve at room temperature with potato chips. (Note: To make garlic vinegar, add 1 clove garlic to wine vinegar and let stand.)

CARAMEL MERINGUE BARS

¾ cup soft butter or margarine
½ cup brown sugar (packed)
½ cup granulated sugar
3 eggs, separated
1 tsp. vanilla
2 cups *sifted* GOLD MEDAL Flour
1 tsp. baking powder
¼ tsp. soda
¼ tsp. salt
6-oz. pkg. chocolate pieces
1 cup flaked or grated coconut
¾ cup coarsely chopped nuts
1 cup brown sugar (packed)

Heat oven to 350° (mod.). Grease an oblong pan, 13x9½x2". Blend butter, ½ cup brown sugar, granulated sugar, egg yolks, and vanilla. Beat 2 min., med. speed on mixer or 300 strokes by hand, scraping bowl constantly. Sift in dry ingredients and stir into creamed mixture until thoroughly mixed. Spread or pat dough in pan. Sprinkle with chocolate pieces, coconut, and nuts. Beat egg whites until frothy; add 1 cup brown sugar and beat until stiff, but not dry. Spread on top of chocolate-coconut-nut mixture. Bake *35 to 40 min.* Cool and cut into bars. *Makes 40 to 60 bars.*

WASSAIL BOWL

Spiced Oranges: Stud 3 oranges with whole cloves (½" apart); place in baking pan with a little water, and bake in slow mod. oven (325°) for *30 min.*

Wassail:

3 qt. apple cider
2 sticks cinnamon, 3" long
½ tsp. nutmeg
½ cup honey
⅓ cup lemon juice
2 tsp. lemon rind
2 no. 2 cans pineapple juice (5 cups)

Heat cider and cinnamon sticks in large saucepan. Bring to boil; simmer covered 5 min. Add remaining ingredients and simmer uncovered 5 min. longer. Pour into punch bowl and float Spiced Oranges on top, using cinnamon sticks for stirring. *40 punch cup servings.*

MYSTERY FRUITCAKE

1 pkg. Betty Crocker Honey Spice or Yellow Cake Mix
4 cups candied mixed fruit (two 1-lb. jars)
½ cup *each* whole red and green candied cherries (½ lb.)
1½ cups seedless raisins (½ lb.)
1 cup dates, cut up (6½-oz. pkg.)
4¼ cups pecan halves (1 lb.)
1 pkg. Betty Crocker Fluffy White Frosting Mix

Make cake as directed on pkg. Cool. Crumble cooled cake into large bowl and add rest of ingredients.

Make Frosting Mix as directed on pkg. and add to the fruit, nuts, and cake mixture. Stir with spoon or toss together with hands until mixture is damp and blended together. PACK TIGHTLY into foil-lined 10" tube pan or two foil-lined 8½x4½x2¾" or 9x5x3" loaf pans. Pat down with buttered hands until smooth. Cover cake with foil and chill in refrigerator *at least* 24 hr. Cake improves if stored longer. Cake should be kept refrigerated. Slice with sharp knife and serve cold. *Makes 6½-lb. fruit-cake.*

Here Comes the Bride

There are many myths and legends about our wedding customs, but we do know that all of them stem from ancient times and from many different countries.

The throwing of rice began among primitive peoples. To them, rice was an emblem of fertility; throwing it after the departing bride and groom expressed the hope of fruitfulness for the union.

In ancient Greece it was the custom to throw flour and sweetmeats over the bridal couple to symbolize an abundance of all that is sweet and good and desirable.

The best man, too, harks back

to primitive times and is un-
doubtedly a survival of the
ancient custom of marriage-
by-capture. The bridegroom
needed a friend to help him
ward off pursuers when he went
after the bride, and that friend
became the "best man."

Brides wore white for purity
and joy, and they wore "something blue" to reveal their love
and fidelity. The Anglo-Saxon
bride was married with her
hair hanging loose as a sign of
freedom; after the wedding she
bound her hair up to show that
she had given up her freedom.
Except for this last custom,
most of the ancient wedding
customs are still observed.

ENGAGEMENT PARTIES

You've just become engaged and you'd love to tell everyone you see. But what fun it is to keep the secret until your announcement party! Here are suggestions for a variety of parties to announce the happy news.

AT TEA TIME

Set your prettiest tea table. With tiny ribbons, tie a heart with the two names on it to each cup handle.

Pink Tea Menu: See p. 87 for menu and suggestions for tea.

ENGAGEMENT LUNCHEON

**Cantaloupe Wedges
with Melon Balls and Berries
Chicken-Rice en Casserole
Two-layer Fruit Gelatin Mold
Hot Biscuits (cut with bell cutter)
Confetti Angel Food Cake**

AT A LUNCHEON FOR THE GIRLS

Have your mother break the news to guests as they arrive. Or you may want to plan a special way of revealing the engagement. But whatever you plan, keep it dignified.

CHICKEN-RICE EN CASSEROLE

**¼ cup chicken fat or butter
5 tbsp. flour
1½ tsp. salt
⅛ tsp. pepper
1 cup seasoned chicken broth
1½ cups milk
1½ cups cooked white or wild rice
   (½ cup uncooked)
2 cups cut-up cooked chicken
¾ cup sliced mushrooms
⅓ cup chopped green pepper
2 tbsp. chopped pimiento
¼ cup slivered almonds**

Heat oven to 350° (mod.). Melt fat in saucepan over low heat. Blend in flour, salt, and pepper. Cook over low heat until smooth and bubbly. Remove from heat. Stir in chicken broth and milk. Bring to boil; boil 1 min., stirring constantly. Mix sauce with remaining ingredients. Pour into greased oblong baking dish, 10x6x1½". Bake *40 to 45 min.* Sprinkle with chopped parsley before serving. *8 servings.*

THE STORY OF THE FIRST BRIDAL SHOWER

Years ago a pretty Dutch girl loved a poor miller—poor because he gave away much of his flour to the needy. The girl's father opposed the match and refused to give her the customary dowry.

Wishing to help the miller who had befriended them, the poor people of the community went to the girl's home and "showered" her with many small gifts. Though modest, all the gifts together surpassed the dowry and made it possible for the young pair to marry. And so they lived happily ever after!

WHAT SORT OF SHOWER?

They may vary from a Linen, China, Glassware, Kitchen, Recipe, or Bathroom Shower to a Lingerie, Handkerchief, Beauty, or Miscellaneous Shower—with the preferences of the bride-to-be always in mind.

A shower may take place at a luncheon, an afternoon tea, a dinner party, an evening party—or even a morning breakfast, or a sewing or knitting bee. Surprise showers are fun. So are coeducational showers —men included!

ETIQUETTE NOTE

A shower is given only by an intimate friend of the bride. It is not proper for a member of the bride's family to give a shower for her. Only good friends of the bride should be invited. This includes the wedding party, and members of the families of the bride and groom.

SHOWER PENNSYLVANIA DUTCH STYLE

The colorful customs and motifs of the Pennsylvania Dutch inspired us to plan a linen shower with a Pennsylvania Dutch theme.

Dowry Chest of Gifts

The dowry chests filled with linens were a great tradition with the Pennsylvania Dutch. The chests were painted and decorated with German script letters.

For a very special way to present the gifts of linens, you might find an old-fashioned chest, line it with a charming floral wallpaper, and paint the exterior a bright color. The wedding date can be printed in German script in a contrasting color. Then present this modern dowry chest filled with gifts from shower guests to the bride-to-be.

The Party Table

Place mats or tray mats may be cut from Pennsylvania Dutch design wallpaper stocked by many stores. Cut the wallpaper with pinking shears, in either the typical rectangular shape or the shape of a heart, a popular Dutch design motif.

Serve a Favorite Dutch Dessert

According to legend, a young Pennsylvania Dutch man was courting a pretty maid but was not sure of her culinary ability. To please him, she created a dessert which was pie, cake, and sauce—all in one. He tasted it, smiled, and said, "Vot a funny cake!" And so they were wed.

Serve:
Chocolate Funny Cake (p. 160)
Coffee

Needles and Pins Gift Wrap

"Needles and pins, needles and pins, when a man marries . . ."

After wrapping your gift, attach a heart-shaped pin cushion in the center of the bow. Fill the cushion with needles and pins. Paint the above lines in gay red brush strokes over entire package. Plain pink shelf paper could make an effective wrap for this package.

FRUIT DUET SALAD

Orange Gelatin Ring

2 pkg. orange-flavored gelatin
2 cups boiling liquid (water or
    fruit juice)
1 pt. orange sherbet
11-oz. can mandarin oranges,
    drained (1 cup)

Dissolve gelatin in boiling liquid. Immediately add orange sherbet and stir until melted. Add oranges. Pour into 1½-qt. ring mold and chill until firm. Unmold and fill center with Ambrosia Fruit Salad (recipe below). *10 to 12 servings.*

Ambrosia Fruit Salad

11-oz. can mandarin oranges,
    drained (1 cup)
13-oz. can pineapple chunks,
    drained (1⅔ cups)
1 cup flaked coconut
1 cup commercial sour cream (or
    ½ cup whipping cream,
    whipped)
1 cup cut-up or miniature
    marshmallows

Mix all ingredients. Chill several hr. or overnight.

Note: Ambrosia Fruit Salad is delicious served separately as a salad or dessert.

For pink or yellow gelatin rings: Substitute raspberry or lemon-flavored gelatin in place of the orange-flavored gelatin, and raspberry or lemon sherbet in place of the orange sherbet. Omit mandarin oranges. Fill with Ambrosia Fruit Salad.

LOBSTER MORNAY

8 to 10 toast cups
¼ cup butter
¼ cup flour
2½ cups milk
⅛ tsp. cayenne
¼ tsp. nutmeg
¾ cup grated processed Swiss
    cheese
¼ cup grated Parmesan cheese
two 5-oz. cans lobster, broken in
    chunks (frozen lobster or
    lobster tails may be used)
¼ tsp. sherry flavoring, if desired

Melt butter over low heat. Stir in flour until well blended. Cook over low heat, stirring until mixture is smooth and bubbly. Remove from heat. Gradually stir in milk. Bring to boil, stirring constantly. Boil 1 min. Blend in seasonings and cheeses. Fold in lobster and sherry. Serve in toast cups, garnished with parsley. *8 to 10 servings.*

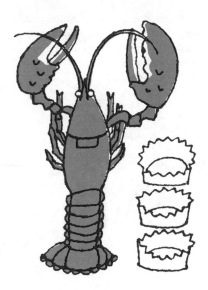

CHOCOLATE FUNNY CAKE

Pastry

1 cup *sifted* GOLD MEDAL Flour
½ tsp. salt
**⅓ cup plus 1 tbsp. hydrogenated
shortening (or ⅓ cup lard)**
2 tbsp. water

Mix flour and salt. Cut in shortening. Sprinkle with water. Mix with fork until all flour is moistened. Round into ball. Roll pastry 1" larger than inverted 9" pie pan. Ease into pan; flute high on edge. Cover with Pliofilm and put aside while preparing sauce and batter.

Chocolate Sauce

**1½ sq. unsweetened chocolate
(1½ oz.)**
½ cup water
⅔ cup sugar
¼ cup butter
1½ tsp. vanilla

Melt chocolate with water; add sugar. Bring to boil, stirring constantly. Remove from heat; stir in butter and vanilla. Set aside.

Cake

1 cup *sifted* GOLD MEDAL Flour
¾ cup sugar
1 tsp. baking powder
½ tsp. salt
¼ cup shortening
½ cup milk
½ tsp. vanilla
1 egg
½ cup finely chopped nuts

Heat oven to 350° (mod.). Sift dry ingredients together. Add shortening, milk, and vanilla. Beat 2 min., med. speed on mixer or 300 vigorous strokes by hand. Scrape sides and bottom of bowl constantly. Add egg. Beat 2 more min., scraping bowl. Pour batter into prepared pie pan. Stir sauce and pour carefully over cake batter. Sprinkle top with nuts. Bake 55 *to* 60 *min.*, or until toothpick stuck in center comes out clean. Serve with whipped cream or ice cream. *8 servings.*

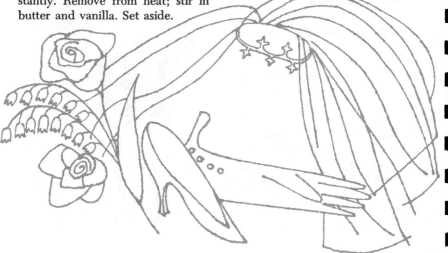

BRIDAL DINNER

This is usually given by the groom's family, although it might be given by any relative or friend. The guests include all members of the bridal party, the families of the bride and groom, and the clergyman and his wife. Because everyone taking part in the wedding is there, it is an ideal time for the wedding rehearsal, either before or after the dinner, at home or at church (wherever the ceremony is to take place).

APPETIZER COURSE
BEFORE BRIDAL DINNER

In the living room before dinner, serve:

**Fruit Punch with Sherbet
Darts and Dips à la Cupid**

DART AND DIPS À LA CUPID

Place your favorite cheese dip mixture in a heart-shaped dish. Surround with crisp shoestring potato straws or pretzel sticks, a few of them sticking out of the dip.

BRIDAL DINNER, BUFFET STYLE

**Turkey-Ham Platter
Scalloped Corn and Oysters
Herb Bread   Watermelon Pickles
Salad of Tossed Greens
and Mandarin Oranges
Strawberry Angel Roll (p. 56)**

TURKEY-HAM PLATTER

Arrange slices of roast turkey and baked ham around a ring of jellied cranberry with whole cranberry sauce in the center.

BRIDAL DINNER, SIT-DOWN STYLE

**Roast Beef
Mashed Potatoes   Broccoli Bouquets
Tomatoes Vinaigrette   Hot Rolls
Cherries Jubilee**

CHERRIES JUBILEE

Melt ¾ cup currant jelly in chafing dish. Add no. 303 can pitted Bing cherries or 2 cups fresh pitted Bing cherries, poached; 1 tbsp. grated orange rind; brandy flavoring to taste. Heat slowly to simmering, stirring occasionally. Serve hot over vanilla ice cream. *8 to 10 servings.*

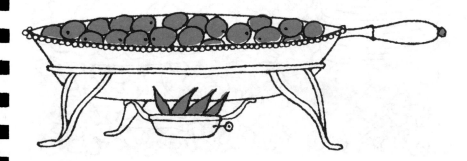

AFTER THE WEDDING REFRESHMENTS

The bridal table is beautiful with snowy lace or linen and gleaming appointments. Its centerpiece and chief ornament is the tiered white-frosted wedding cake. The table may be set for "sit-down" or "stand-up" refreshments depending upon the number of guests, time of day, and the wishes of the bride's parents (who are the hosts).

Delicious is the wedding repast, whether simple or elaborate. When planning a reception, remember that the menu depends on the time of day. Breakfast is served during the morning hours until 12:30 p.m. From 12:30 until 2 p.m., choose a luncheon menu. Tea refreshments are appropriate from 2 until 6 p.m. and at receptions after 8 in the evening. Plan a buffet supper if the reception falls between 6 and 8 o'clock.

EARLY WEDDING BREAKFAST

Wedding Day Fruit Punch
Eggs Benedict
Crisp Watermelon Pickles
Elegant Salad of Greens and
Artichoke Hearts
Ice Cream Molds   Wedding Cake

EGGS BENEDICT

For each serving, cover a round of split and toasted English muffin (or toast) with a thin slice of fried ham (same size) or spread with deviled ham. Top each with a poached egg and cover with hollandaise sauce. Serve at once.

LATE WEDDING BREAKFAST

Sea Food Casseroles
or
**Baked Sweetbreads and Mushrooms
on Ham**
Lemon-buttered Asparagus Tips
Fancy Relish Tray
Assorted Hot Rolls
Fruit Ices   Easy Petits Fours

EASY PETITS FOURS

Heat oven to 350° (mod.). Make batter as directed on any flavor Betty Crocker Cake Mix pkg.—*except* Angel Food and Chiffon. Spread in greased and floured jelly roll pan, 15½x10½x1″. Bake *20 to 22 min.* Cool in pan. Mix Betty Crocker Fluffy White Frosting Mix as directed on pkg. Divide into small bowls; tint. Frost cake sections with different colors. Cut in diamond, square, and triangle shapes. Trim with rosettes, chopped nuts, silver shot, gumdrops, candy sprinkles, chocolate pieces, or maraschino cherries.

BAKED SWEETBREADS AND MUSHROOMS

Divide cooked sweetbreads into serving-size pieces. Roll in seasoned flour and pan-fry in 3 tbsp. butter until light brown. Place in baking dish. Sauté ½ lb. sliced mushrooms in 3 tbsp. butter; then make medium white sauce in the pan using 1½ cups milk. Pour over sweetbreads. Bake in mod. oven (350°) *30 min.* Serve on rounds of toast or thin ham or Canadian bacon slices. *1 lb. sweetbreads serves 5 to 6.*

SEA FOOD CASSEROLES

½ cup butter
⅓ cup flour
1 tsp. salt
¼ cup minced parsley
2 tsp. grated onion
2 tsp. lemon juice
few drops Tabasco sauce
2 cups milk
2 egg yolks, slightly beaten
1 cup flaked crabmeat
1 cup chopped lobster
1 cup chopped, cooked, cleaned
   shrimp
2 egg whites, beaten
⅔ cup buttered bread crumbs

Heat oven to 350° (mod.). Melt butter in saucepan over low heat. Blend in flour and seasonings. Cook over low heat, stirring until mixture is smooth and bubbly. Remove from heat. Stir in milk. Bring to boil; boil 1 min., stirring constantly. Remove from heat, stir in egg yolks. Bring to boil again, stirring constantly. Remove from heat and add sea food. Fold in beaten egg whites and spoon hot mixture into shells or individual baking dishes. Top with crumbs and sprinkle with paprika. Bake *20 min. Makes 16 servings in shells, 10 in casserole.*

WEDDING SUPPER

Chicken Salad with Green Grapes
or
Sea Food Salad with Grapefruit
Tiny Hot Biscuits
Ice Cream in Wedding Molds
Petits Fours

PARTY CHICKEN SALAD WITH GREEN GRAPES

Toss together 2 cups cut-up cold cooked chicken (large chunks), 1 cup cut-up celery (½" pieces), 1 tbsp. lemon juice, salt and pepper to taste. Mix in ½ cup mayonnaise and carefully fold in 1 cup halved green grapes. Arrange mounds of salad in lettuce cups or in tomato flower cups. *6 servings.*

SEA FOOD SALAD

Garnish your favorite sea food salad (perhaps a combination of shrimp, crabmeat, and salmon) with *fresh* grapefruit sections.

COFFEE FOR FORTY

Mix 1 egg (shell and all) into 1 lb. coffee. Add 1 cup cold water. Tie coffee in cheesecloth bag large enough to allow room for coffee to swell. Measure 7 qt. cold water into large coffee pot. Immerse coffee bag in water; bring to boil. Remove pot from heat. Leave bag of coffee in water 3 to 4 min.; remove and stir. Keep hot. If preferred, use boiling water to start; bring to boil. Stir. Remove from heat. Let stand 10 min. Remove coffee and serve.

WEDDING RECEPTIONS

June Punch
Ice Cream Balls
Wedding Cake   Groom's Cake
Salted Nuts   Coffee

JUNE PUNCH

4 cups sugar
4 cups water
2 cups strong black tea
six 6-oz. cans frozen lemonade
  concentrate, undiluted
two 6-oz. cans frozen orange juice
  concentrate, undiluted
2 no. 2 cans pineapple juice
  (5 cups)
2 cups cut-up fresh strawberries
  and juice or 16 oz. frozen
  strawberries, thawed
1 gal. water
2 qt. dry ginger ale

Make syrup by boiling sugar and 4 cups water 10 min. Add tea and fruit juices. Chill 2 to 3 hr. Add remaining ingredients. Pour over block of ice in punch bowl or over ice cubes. *60 to 70 servings.*

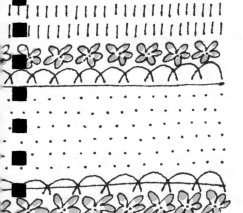

GLAMOUR DECORATIONS FOR WEDDING CAKES

Dot with shining silver candies— lovely in candlelight.

Perhaps you will want to use tiny, fresh flowers on the cake frosting and around edge of cake plate.

A traditional wedding bell, a bride and groom, or a miniature bouquet of real flowers can top the cake.

GROOM'S CAKE

Cut any dark fruit cake into tiny squares. Wrap them up for the guests to dream on.

WEDDING RECEPTION
WITH A FRENCH FLAIR

Golden Punch
Petits Choux (Tiny Tea Puffs p. 87)
| Olives | Radishes |
| Bon Bon Cookies | Cream Wafers |

Tiered Wedding Cake
| Coffee | Tea |

TIERED WEDDING CAKE
USING SILVER WHITE CAKE

Use two double recipes Silver White Cake *(below)*, beating 2½ min. each mixing time. Bake in two 12" layers, two 9" layers, and two 6" layers, using times at right. Assemble and decorate.

SILVER WHITE CAKE

2¼ cups sifted SOFTASILK Cake Flour
1½ cups sugar
3½ tsp. baking powder
1 tsp. salt
½ cup soft shortening
1 cup milk
1 tsp. flavoring
4 egg whites unbeaten

Heat oven to 350° (mod.). Grease generously and flour two layer pans, 8 or 9x1½", or an oblong pan, 13x9½-x2". Sift flour, sugar, baking powder, and salt into bowl. Add shortening, ⅔ of the milk, and flavoring. Beat 2 min., med. speed on mixer or 300 vigorous strokes by hand. Scrape sides and bottom of bowl constantly. Add rest of milk and egg whites. Beat 2 more min., scraping bowl frequently. Pour into prepared pans. Bake *layers 30 to 35 min., oblong 35 to 40 min.*, or until cake tests done. Cool.

TIERED WEDDING CAKE

Baking the Cake: Grease generously three layer pans. Use one 12" layer, one 10" layer, and one 8" layer. Line bottoms with heavy *brown* paper; grease paper and flour. *Heat oven to 350°* (mod.). Make batter with *two* pkg. Betty Crocker White Cake Mix. Follow pkg. directions— *except* use 2¼ cups water, 4 egg whites plus 1 whole egg. Increase mixing time by 1½ (total of 6 min.). Pour about 5½ cups of batter into 12" pan and refrigerate. Pour about 4 cups of batter into 10" pan and 2 cups into 8" pan. Place 10" layer near rear of oven and 8" near front. Bake *10" layer 30 to 35 min.; 8" layer 25 to 30 min.* Cool 10 min.; remove from pans. Place 12" layer in center of oven. Bake *30 to 40 min.* Cool 10 min. and remove from pan.

Repeat above directions, using two more pkg. of White Cake Mix. Frost with Betty Crocker Creamy White or Fluffy White Frosting Mix.

Putting the cake together: Put one 12" layer on a large plate or mirror. Frost top; put on other 12" layer. Frost sides and top, swirling icing to make decorative sides and edges. Cut a 10" cardboard circle; place on top of frosted layers. Place one 10" layer on cardboard; frost top. Put on second 10" layer; frost sides and top, swirling the icing. Cut an 8" cardboard circle; place on top of frosted layers. Follow above directions for 8" layers. *Serves about 70.*

EASY BRIDE'S CAKE

This attractive bride's cake is easily made with 2 pkg. Betty Crocker White Cake Mix and 4 pkg. Betty Crocker Creamy White Frosting Mix.

To Bake: Heat oven to 350° (mod.). Grease and flour a jelly roll pan, 15½x10½x1". Make batter as directed on pkg. Pour into prepared pan. Bake *20 to 22 min.* Remove from pan and cool. Repeat for second cake.

To Assemble: Cut both cakes into fourths crosswise. Make Thin Glaze (Blend 2 pkg. frosting mix, ½ cup hot water, and ¼ cup light corn syrup. Beat until smooth by hand or mixer.) Frost tops of cake strips; stack layers by twos. This will make 4 double-layer cakes. Add 1 to 2 tbsp. hot water to remaining icing to make it very thin. Frost sides of cakes; let set until hardened, about ½ hr.

To Decorate: Mix 2 pkg. frosting mix, ⅓ cup soft white shortening, ½ cup hot water, almond flavoring to taste. Frost tops and sides of cake, saving some frosting for decorating. Tint remaining frosting pale pink. Using cake decorating tube with rosette point, pipe around top edges of cakes and make crossed lines of tiny frosting peaks on cake tops. Other decorations may be made, as desired.

To Arrange: Arrange cakes in a square with inside corners touching on a large tray or large piece of doily-covered cardboard. Fill center with white and pastel pink flowers and tall white candles. Tuck greens, such as boxwood, around the edge of cake.

To Serve: Slice each cake in half lengthwise; then in about 12 pieces. *Makes 96 small servings.*

If you wish, extra cakes may be decorated and set in to replace the original ones that are cut and served.

Cakes may be baked the day before they are decorated if tightly covered during storage.

GOLDEN PUNCH

2 cups lemon juice
2 cups orange juice
2 cups sugar
2 cups water
4 qt. ginger ale, chilled

Combine juices, sugar, and water in large pitcher or bowl. Let stand 30 min. When ready to serve, add ginger ale. Serve in punch bowl with decorated ice ring. *32 to 40 servings.*

WEDDING ANNIVERSARIES

Warm hospitality, together with pleasant memories, make a wedding anniversary the occasion for a delightful party which may be given by relatives, friends, or the couple themselves in their own home. Whether formal or informal, the type of party chosen will depend upon the wishes and the health of the honored guests.

PLANNING AN ANNIVERSARY PARTY

Decide whether it will be a formal or informal party. If a large group is to be invited, a double reception may be the best arrangement—"three to five" and "after eight o'clock". Plan whether extra help will be needed; plan who will pour, and then invite early; plan ample refrigerator storage and serving space. Prepare all food that can be made ahead of time. Order early: invitations, flower arrangements, ice creams, cakes, candies, nuts, and other foods.

INVITATIONS

These may be informal, by note or phone. If the party or dinner is formal, invitations should be engraved in silver or gold on white paper. A charming touch would be a copy of the original wedding invitation and below it the invitation to the anniversary celebration.

DOWN MEMORY LANE

With the invitation include a sheet of heavy white paper with the heading: "Do You Remember?" Ask older friends to write an anecdote from the early years of the honored couple on it. Tie these together with a silver or gold ribbon and present with a book in which the guests will offer best wishes and congratulations.

WEDDING ANNIVERSARIES

Year	Symbol
1st	paper
2nd	cotton
3rd	leather
4th	silk, fruit, flowers
5th	wood
6th	iron
7th	copper, bronze, brass
8th	electrical appliances, rubber
9th	pottery
10th	tin, aluminum
15th	crystal
20th	china
25th	silver
30th	pearl
40th	ruby
50th	gold
75th	diamond

TABLE DECORATIONS

For the Silver Wedding Anniversary:
A silver-grey cloth with a mound of pink roses, baby's breath, and sprays of asparagus fern would be very lovely. Narrow pink satin streamers with silver bells (foil) radiate from this centerpiece. Use silver candlesticks or candelabra with tall white or pink candles.

For the Golden Anniversary: Use lace cloth over gold, with crystal vases of pale yellow roses. Matching yellow candles in crystal or softly gleaming brass candleholders, and a yellow rosebud by each place card would be a breath-taking picture for the golden years.

For the Silver or Golden Anniversary: Use a white rayon-satin or damask cloth. Half-blown white roses with fronds of maidenhair fern, silver or gold Christmas tree balls, and tall pale green candles buried in the flowers make a dainty and beautiful centerpiece. For directions for making silver or gold leaves, see p. 60

TABLE SERVICE

Punch may be served at a small table or at the opposite end of a large table where coffee is being served. If on a small table, surround punch bowl with colorful artificial grapes arranged around the bottom with ropes of smilax.

One or two coffee and tea services may be used. Two patterns of china or glass are permissible for a large gathering.

Coffee and tea are served at one end of the table, punch at the other.

MAKE A "MONEY TREE"

If friends wish to make a gift of money, use a small, thick evergreen for the centerpiece. Wrap silver dollars in foil and hang on the tree. If not available, buy silver or gold-wrapped "money" at candy counter. With a gift card bearing donors' names, present an equivalent amount of real money to the couple.

ANNIVERSARY BUFFETS

Anniversary Fruit Tray
Crispy Cheese Foldovers
Buttered Nut Bread Rounds
Twin Hearts Wedding Cakes
Individual Ice Cream Molds
Bon Bons   Salted Nuts
Coffee   Tea   Punch

Party Chicken Salad
with Green Grapes (p. 164)
Assorted Rolls   Green and Ripe Olives
Fancy Cakes
Mint Wafers   Salted Nuts
Coffee   Tea   Punch

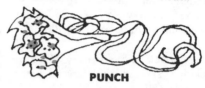

ANNIVERSARY FRUIT TRAY

Arrange on a bed of greens on silver tray: minted pineapple spears, peach halves centered with cream cheese nut balls, pear halves centered with fresh chopped mint or candied ginger, and bananas rolled in chopped salted nuts and cut in 2" slices.

CRISPY CHEESE FOLDOVERS

Prepare 1 stick Betty Crocker Instant Mixing Pie Crust Mix as directed on pkg.—*except before* adding liquid, mix in ½ cup grated Cheddar cheese. Roll out into 12x 10" rectangle; cut into thirty 2" squares. Brush with butter and sprinkle with poppy, sesame, or caraway seeds. Fold into triangles, seal with floured fork, brush with butter, and sprinkle with seeds. Bake on ungreased baking sheet *8 min.*, or until lightly browned.

TWIN HEARTS WEDDING CAKES

Bake large twin hearts and individual heart cakes. Decorate with white icing and silver dragées. Serve small cakes on silver trays.

PUNCH

Raspberry-pineapple or strawberry-pineapple frozen juices may be mixed with carbonated beverages, sparkling water, or ginger ale and served with Decorative Ice Ring.

DECORATIVE ICE RING FOR THE PUNCH BOWL

Arrange lemon slices and quarters, red and green maraschino cherries, and sprigs of mint or huckleberry in bottom of ring mold. Add enough water to partially cover. Freeze. When frozen, add water to fill ¾ full. Freeze. Unmold; float fruit-side-up on punch in punch bowl.

RECEPTION REQUIREMENTS FOR 100 GUESTS

18 qt. salad
12 doz. rolls
10 pt. green olives
4 large cans ripe olives
11 doz. fancy cakes
4 lb. bon bons
4 lb. salted nuts
3 lb. coffee
1 gal. cream
1 pkg. sugar

SUBJECT INDEX

RECIPE INDEX